They Who Tarry

The Doctrine of Translated Beings

R. Clayton Brough

Horizon Publishers

INTERNATIONAL STANDARD BOOK NUMBER
0-88290-069-2

LIBRARY OF CONGRESS CATALOG CARD NUMBER
76-29255

Printed in the
United States of America
by

HORIZON
PUBLISHERS
Post Office Box 490
55 East 300 South
Bountiful, Utah 84010
292-1959

EXPRESSION OF APPRECIATION

The author would like to express sincere appreciation to Dr. Dale J. Stevens, Associate Professor of Geography at Brigham Young University, for his assistance and critical comments as to the contents of this book.

Also, deep thankfulness is expressed to Duane S. Crowther, President of Horizon Publishers, who expertly assisted this writer by making several helpful suggestions in readying this book for publication.

And last but most important, I would like to publicly thank the Lord for His kindness in inspiring me in this research effort; and also thank my lovely wife, Ethel, who has continually sustained, encouraged and assisted me during my many hours of writing and revisions.

R. Clayton Brough

To

Alison and Richard

PREFACE

To members of The Church of Jesus Christ of Latter-day Saints, the subject of "translation" and "translated beings" has always been intriguing. Since the early days of the Church, Prophets, Presidents, and General Authorities of the Kingdom of God upon the earth have spoken on the subject of translation, and about those individuals who scripture records as having been translated. Whenever questions about the subject of translation have been raised, the Brethren have endeavored to answer them with as much information as the scriptures can supply and with as much knowledge, gained through inspiration, as the Lord has felt appropriate they should give.

The subject of translation and translated beings is not a "mystery," by any means. There is enough adequate information presented in the scriptures and in discourses by Church leaders that those questions which are most often asked by Latter-day Saints about the subject of translation can be answered quite satisfactorily. Because these questions are still being asked today, and stories about translated beings are being circulated with seemingly more frequency, this writer has felt it would be beneficial to bring together into book form some of the most comprehensive and firsthand information that is presently available on the subject.

The reader should be aware that this is not an official Church publication and that this writer is solely responsible for the manner in which documented material is presented within this book. It is appropriate that those who read this book seek inspiration from the Holy Ghost as to the truthfulness of the information contained herein.

R. Clayton Brough

TABLE OF CONTENTS

CHAPTER 1

THE NATURE OF TRANSLATED BEINGS

The Doctrine of Translation

Since the time of Adam, faithful members of the Lord's Church have been permitted in various dispensations of time to either prolong their existence upon this earth, free from any physical suffering, or to be taken into heavenly realms without immediately tasting death. In a term familiar to most Latter-day Saints, these people are said to have been "translated."

According to the Prophet Joseph Smith, the doctrine of translation is that it is a "power" exercised through the Melchizedek Priesthood, and that the keys to that power have often been held by righteous men throughout the various dispensations of mankind.[1] The Prophet has said:

> Now the doctrine of translation is a power which belongs to this [the Melchizedek] priesthood. There are many things which belong to the powers of the priesthood and the keys thereof, that have been kept hid from before the foundation of the world; they are hid from the wise and prudent to be revealed in the last times.
>
> Many have supposed that the doctrine of translation was a doctrine whereby men were taken immediately into the presence of God, and into an eternal fulness, but this is a mistaken idea. Their place of habitation is that of the terrestrial order, and a place prepared for such characters he held in reserve to be ministering angels unto many planets, and who as yet have not

---

1. Joseph Smith, *(The Documentary) History of the Church* (Deseret Book Company, Salt Lake City, Utah, 1946-1951), Volume 4, pp. 209-210.

*entered into so great a fulness as those who are resur-
rected from the dead.*[1]

President John Taylor has similarly stated that the power of
translation "is one of the principles of the gospel," and "will
exist in the last days" when the "Zion of the latter days" has
been built:

> We are told in the scripture—which is a meagre
> account of it, that—"Enoch was not, for God took
> him." And we may add, Enoch's city and Enoch's
> people were not, for God took them; they were trans-
> lated. *The principle of translation was a principle that
> at that time existed in the Church, and is one of the
> principles of the gospel, and which will exist in the
> last day.*[2]

And also,

> The [Church] organization which we possess to-
> day was gradually effected, which is as full and com-
> plete, perhaps as ever existed upon the earth. How
> perfect it was in the days of Enoch we are not told,
> but *everything that they had revealed to them pertain-
> ing to the organization of the Church of God, also
> pertaining to doctrine and ordinances, we have had
> revealed to us, excepting one thing, and that is the
> principle and power of translation; that, however, will
> in due time be restored also.* And if they in their day
> built a Zion, we have one to build in our day, and when
> this shall be done and everything is in readiness, the
> *Zion which the people of Enoch built and which was
> translated, will descend from above, and the Zion of
> the latter days which this people will build, will ascend
> by virtue of this principle and power, and the former
> and the latter-day Zion will meet each other,* and the

---

1. *Ibid.*
2. John Taylor, *Journal of Discourses*, Volume 26, p. 90.

dwellers in both will embrace and kiss each other, so we are told in the revelations of God.[1]

Apparently, like any principle of the gospel that is effectively learned and incorporated into a person's life and soul, the power of translation is most vividly understood when it is taught through the inspiration of the Spirit of the Lord to those individuals who are spiritually capable of receiving such instruction. Elder Orson Pratt, when once speaking of the translation of Enoch and the people of the City of Enoch, mentioned that because of the righteousness and preparedness of that group of saints "they were instructed and taught" in all of the Lord's ways, "and among other things they learned the great doctrine and principle of translation." The following statement is that of Elder Pratt:

Our new revelations that we have received inform us of a great many individuals that were translated before the flood. We read that a great and mighty Prophet of the Most High God was sent forth in the days of Adam, namely Enoch, the seventh generation from Adam, who lived contemporary with his ancestor Adam; that in his days a great number of people heard the plan of salvation preached to them by the power of the Holy Ghost that rested upon Enoch and those who were called with him; that they received this plan of salvation and gathered themselves out from among the various nations of the earth where they had obeyed the Gospel; that they were instructed, after they assembled in one, in righteousness, for three hundred and sixty-five years; that they learned the laws of the kingdom, and concerning God and every principle of righteousness that was necessary to enable them to enter into the fulness of the glory of heaven; they were instructed to build up a city, and it was called a city of holiness, for God came down and dwelt with that people; he was in their midst, they beheld his glory, they

---

1. *Ibid.*, Volume 23, pp. 32-33.

saw his face, and he condescended to dwell among them for many long years, during which time they were instructed and taught in all of his ways, and among other things *they learned the great doctrine and principle of translation, for that is a doctrine the same as the doctrine of the resurrection of the dead, which is among the first principles of the plan of salvation; and we may also say that the doctrine of translation, which is intimately connected with that of the resurrection, is also one of the first principles of the doctrine of Christ.* They were instructed in relation to this government, the object of it, etc.

According to the light and knowledge which the Latter-day Saints have upon this subject, revealed in the revelations given through Joseph Smith, we find that *those people, when they were fully prepared, having learned the doctrine of translation, were caught up into the heavens, the whole city, the people and their habitations.*[1]

The Characteristics of Translated Beings

The characteristics of translated beings are such that their mortal bodies are changed so that their life is prolonged and any physical suffering is eliminated. They are neither mortal nor immortal, neither resurrected nor exalted. They are, in the words of the Prophet Joseph Smith, in a state of translated existence which temporarily frees them "from the tortures and sufferings of the body." Concerning this physical nature of translation, the Prophet stated:

Now it was evident that there was a better resurrection, or else God would not have revealed it unto Paul. Wherein then, can it be said a better resurrection? This distinction is made between the doctrine of the actual resurrection and translation: *translation obtains deliverance from the tortures and sufferings of the*

---

1. Orson Pratt, *Journal of Discourses*, Volume 17, pp. 146-149.

body, but their existence will prolong as to the labors and toils of the ministry, before they can enter into so great a rest and glory.

On the other hand, those who were tortured, not accepting deliverance, received an immediate rest from their labors. "And I heard a voice from heaven, saying unto me, Write, Blessed are the dead which die in the Lord, from henceforth: Yea, saith the Spirit, that they may rest from their labours; and their works do follow them." (Rev. 14:13.) *They [translated beings] rest from their labors for a long time, and yet their work is held in reserve for them, that they are permitted to do the same work, after they receive a resurrection of their bodies.*[1]

From the account of the translation of the three Nephites in the Book of Mormon, additional knowledge concerning the characteristics of translated beings is given. We are told, for example, that translated individuals apparently undergo *"a change wrought upon their bodies"* so that they might not suffer pain or "sorrow save it be for the sins of the world," and that they are holy men *"sanctified in the flesh"* insomuch that Satan has "no power over them," and that the powers of the earth cannot hold them. Therefore, this would seem to indicate that translated beings are free of all sin, and are freed from all mortal diseases, sicknesses, sufferings, and the need for constant nourishment. Neither can they be retained, hindered, or slowed down by any earthly physical feature or geographical distance.[2]

As to the specific bodily composition of translated beings, one may only speculate, for information is simply not available. However, it is possible that physical differences between translated beings and mortal beings may not be easily distinguishable to the mortal eye since some Latter-day

---

1. Joseph Smith, *op. cit.*, Volume 4, pp. 209-210.
2. *The Book of Mormon*, 3 Nephi 28.
   Spencer W. Kimball, *The Miracle of Forgiveness* (Bookcraft, Inc., Salt Lake City, Utah, 1969), p. 335.

Saint writers have referred to Paul's statement that "some have entertained angels unawares" (Heb. 13:2) as having possible reference to translated beings who could have visited mortal men, but whose translated state was undetectable by human scrutiny.[1]

Translated Beings And Death

In 1874, Elder Orson Pratt made the following statement:

If we, by study or research, could discover some method or principle by which we could remain in this world and live in this tabernacle forever, we should be willing to do so with all the inconveniences of the present order of things, and still be joyful in our hearts. If any man could by research or learning discover some kind of a way, or means or medicine that would give immortality to the children of men, even in their present state, he would be considered one of the greatest men that ever lived, and the one who had bestowed the greatest blessing upon his fellow-creatures; he would be lauded to the very skies, and his name would be handed down among all people and nations as one of the greatest benefactors of mankind; so earnestly do we feel to cling to life and desire to live, that we would be very willing to put up with the inconveniences of the present state if we could only remain and the monster death have no power over us. But it is in the order of God that man should die. Man brought this upon himself by transgressing the laws of heaven. By putting forth his hand and partaking of that which God has forbidden, he brought this great evil into the world. Death not only came upon our first parents, who committed the first great transgression, but the curse has been inherited by all their generations. None can escape the curse so far as the mortal body is concerned.[2]

---

1. Duane S. Crowther, *Life Everlasting* (Bookcraft, Inc., Salt Lake City, Utah, 1967), p. 124.

2. Orson Pratt, *Journal of Discourses*, Volume 17, p. 146.

Likewise, neither can translated beings escape mortal death. All translated individuals who have been or are now still in the state of translation must, after they have fulfilled their mission upon this earth or elsewhere, undergo a change equivalent to death. The Prophet Joseph Smith has said:

> *Translated bodies cannot enter into rest until they have undergone a change equivalent to death.*[1]

However, the kind of death to which translated beings shall be subjected shall be a change performed "in the twinkling of an eye from mortality to immortality," never having to endure "the pains of death."[2] In regards to this change of death which shall fall upon all those who have been or are now translated, the Savior, in speaking to three of His twelve Nephite disciples who had requested to be translated shortly after He had established His church upon the American continent, said:

> Therefore, more blessed are ye, for *ye shall never taste of death; but ye shall live to behold all the doings of the Father unto the children of men,* even until all things shall be fulfilled according to the will of the Father, when I shall come in my glory with the powers of Heaven.
>
> *And ye shall never endure the pains of death; but when I shall come in my glory ye shall be changed in the twinkling of an eye from mortality to immortality;* and then shall ye be blessed in the kingdom of my Father.
>
> And again, *ye shall not have pain while ye shall dwell in the flesh, neither sorrow* save it be for the sins of the world; and all this will I do because of the thing which ye have desired that ye might bring the souls of men unto me, while the world shall stand.
>
> And for this cause *ye shall have fulness of joy;* and ye shall sit down in the kingdom of my Father; yea,

---

1. Joseph Smith, *op. cit.*, Volume 4, p. 425.
2. *The Book of Mormon*, 3 Nephi 28: 7-10.

your joy shall be full, even as the Father hath given me fulness of joy; and ye shall be even as I am, and I am even as the Father; and the Father and I are one.[1]

And later, Mormon, who wondered about this same question as to whether translated beings need undergo death, received the following answer from the Lord:

> But behold, since I wrote, I have inquired of the Lord, and he hath made it manifest unto me that *there must needs be a change wrought upon their bodies, or else it needs be that they must taste of death;*
> Therefore, that they might not taste of death *there was a change wrought upon their bodies, that they might not suffer pain nor sorrow* save it were for the sins of the world.
> *Now this change was not equal to that which shall take place at the last day;* but there was a change wrought upon them, insomuch that *Satan could have no power over them; and they were sanctified in the flesh,* that they were holy, and that the powers of the earth could not hold them.
> *And in this state they were to remain until the judgement day of Christ; and at that day they were to receive a greater change,* and to be received into the kingdom of the Father to go no more out, but to dwell with God eternally in the heavens.[2]

Concerning this same subject President Joseph Fielding Smith has written:

> If we would only think, we would realize that translated beings are still mortal and will have to pass through the experience of death, or the separation of the spirit and the body, although this will be instantaneous, for the people of the City of Enoch, Elijah,

---

1. *Ibid.*
2. *Ibid.*, 3 Nephi 28:37-40.

and others who received this great blessing in ancient times, before the coming of our Lord, could not have received the resurrection, or the change from mortality to immortality, because our Lord had not paid the debt which frees us from mortality and grants to us the resurrection and immortal life. Christ is the "resurrection and the life," and the "first fruits of them that slept," therefore none could pass from mortality to immortality until our Savior completed his work for the redemption of man and had gained the keys of the resurrection, being the first to rise having "life in himself" and the power to lay down his life and take it up again, thus freeing all men from the bondage which the fall had placed upon them.[1]

The Purposes and Work of Translated Beings

In the words of the Prophet Joseph Smith, the main purpose of translated beings is so that they may act as *"ministering angels unto many planets."*[2] Therefore, not only are translated beings "ministering angels," assigned to fulfill various functions and responsibilities to the inhabitants of this earth, but are also ministers unto the inhabitants of other worlds which the Lord has likewise created. In discussing the roles, responsibilities and work of "ministering angels," the Prophet Moroni mentioned that they declare "the word of Christ" and "bear testimony of him:"

They [ministering angels] are subject unto him to minister according to the word of his command, *showing themselves unto them of strong faith and a firm mind in every form of godliness. And the office of their ministry is to call men unto repentance, and to fulfill and to do the work of the covenants of the Father*, which he hath made unto the children of men, by

---

1. Joseph Fielding Smith, *Answers to Gospel Questions* (Deseret Book Company, Salt Lake City, Utah, 1957), Volume 1, pp. 163-165.
2. Joseph Smith, *op. cit.*, Volume 4, pp. 209-210.

declaring the word of Christ unto the chosen vessels of the Lord, that they may bear testimony of him.[1]

And the Prophet Mormon, particularly speaking about the three Nephites who had been translated, mentions that they "minister...unto all nations, kindreds, tongues and people" to "bring out of them unto Jesus many souls:"

> And it shall come to pass when the Lord seeth fit in his wisdom that *they [the Three Nephites] shall minister unto all the scattered tribes of Israel, and unto all nations, kindreds, tongues and people, and shall bring out of them unto Jesus many souls*, that their desire may be fulfilled, and also because of the convincing power of God which is in them.
>
> And they are as the angels of God, and *if they shall pray unto the Father in the name of Jesus they can show themselves unto whatsoever man it seemeth them good.*
>
> Therefore, great and marvelous works shall be wrought by them, before the great and coming day when all people must surely stand before the judgment-seat of Christ;
>
> Yea even among the Gentiles shall there be a great and marvelous work wrought by them, before that judgment day.
>
> And if ye had all the scriptures which give an account of all the marvelous works of Christ, ye would according to the words of Christ, know that these things must surely come.[2]

There is apparently another definite purpose the Lord had for having translated beings assigned to His various creations. In regards to this earth, President Harold B. Lee has suggested that translated beings have possibly served as the Lord's priesthood representatives upon the earth, often

---

1. *The Book of Mormon*, Moroni 7:30-31.
2. *Ibid.*, 3 Nephi 28:29-31.

to hold Satan in check, particularly during the periods of apostasy which followed each of the dispensations of the gospel:

> President Clark said something that startled some folks years ago. He said, *"It is my faith that the gospel plan has always been here, that His priesthood has always been here, that His priesthood has been here on the earth, and that it will continue to be so until the end comes."* When the conference session was over there were many who said, "My goodness, doesn't President Clark realize that there have been periods of apostasy following each dispensation of the gospel?"
>
> I walked over to the Church Office Building with President Joseph Fielding Smith and he said, *"I believe there has never been a moment of time since the creation but what there has been someone holding the priesthood on the earth to hold Satan in check."* And then I thought of Enoch's city with perhaps thousands who were taken into heaven and were translated. They must have been translated for a purpose and may have sojourned with those living on the earth ever since that time. I have thought of Elijah—and perhaps Moses, for all we know; they were translated beings, as was John the Revelator. I have thought of the three Nephites. Why were they translated and permitted to tarry? For what purpose? An answer was suggested when I heard President Smith, whom we have considered one of our well-informed theologians, make the above statement. *Now that doesn't mean that the kingdom of God has always been present, because these men did not have the authority to administer the saving ordinances of the gospel to the world.* But these individuals were translated for a purpose known to the Lord. There is no question but what they were here.[1]

---

1. Harold B. Lee, *Stand Ye In Holy Places* (Deseret Book Company, Salt Lake City, Utah, 1974), pp. 161-162.

And President Joseph Fielding Smith has likewise written:

> The Lord, of necessity, has kept authorized servants on the earth bearing the priesthood from the days of Adam to the present time; in fact, *there has never been a moment from the beginning that there were not men on the earth holding the Holy Priesthood.* (Moses 5:59.) Even in the days of apostasy, and apostasy has occurred several times, *the Lord never surrendered this earth and permitted Satan to have complete control.* Even when the great apostasy occurred following the death of the Savior's apostles, our Father in heaven held control and had duly authorized servants on the earth to direct his work and to check, to some extent at least, the ravages and corruption of the evil powers. These servants were not permitted to organize the Church nor to officiate in the ordinances of the gospel, but they did check the advances of evil as far as the Lord deemed it necessary. This truth is made manifest in the statement of the Lord in the Doctrine and Covenants wherein the following appears:

>> Wherefore, I will that all men shall repent, for all are under sin, except those which I have reserved unto myself, holy men that ye know not of. (D & C 49:8.)

> *We know that John the Revelator and the three Nephites were granted the privilege of remaining on the earth in the translated state, to "bring souls unto Christ."* We know that this was the request of John and likewise the desire of the three Nephites. [See D & C 7; 3 Nephi 28:4-18.]

> It is reasonable to believe that they were engaged in this work as far as the Lord permitted them to go during these years of spiritual darkness. There are legends and stories which seem to be authentic, showing that these holy messengers were busy among the nations of the earth, and men have been entertained

by them unawares. (Heb. 13:2.) We may also well believe that these translated prophets have always been busy keeping constraint upon the acts of men and nations unbeknown to mortal man.

Translated beings have not passed through death; that is, they have not had the separation of the spirit and the body. This must wait until the coming of the Savior. In the meantime they are busy fulfilling their glorious mission in preparing the way for the elders of Israel to go forth with the message of salvation in all parts of the world.[1]

Those Who Have Been Translated

From scriptural accounts and inferences the following list of people or groups of people appear to have been translated:[2]

1. Enoch and his city. (See Gen. 5:24; Heb. 11:5; Moses 7:18-21, 31, 63, 69; D & C 38:4; 45:11-14.)

2. Many Saints between the time of Enoch and Melchizedek. (Moses 7:27; *Inspired Version of the Bible*, Gen. 14:30-34.)

3. Moses. (Al. 45:18-19; Mt. 17:1-6; *History of the Church*, Vol. 3:387.)

4. Elijah. (2 Kings 2:11; Mt. 17:1-6; *History of the Church*, Vol. 3:387.)

5. Alma the Younger. (Al. 45:18-19.)

6. Nephi, the Son of Helaman. (3 Nephi 1:3.)

---

1. Joseph Fielding Smith, *Answers...*, *op. cit.*, Volume 3, pp. 45-46.
2. Duane S. Crowther, *op. cit.*, pp. 123-124.
   Bruce R. McConkie, *Mormon Doctrine* (Bookcraft, Inc., Salt Lake City, Utah, 1966), pp. 804-808.

All these above translated beings "were with Christ in His resurrection." (D & C 133:53-55.) Therefore, they are now resurrected, not translated. Since the resurrection of the Savior other individuals have been translated and therefore may still be on the earth or elsewhere in a translated form. They include the following:

7. John the Revelator. (Mt. 16:28; John 21:21-23; D & C 7; 3 Nephi 28:6-8.)

8. Some Saints living in the Old World during the early Christian Era, following the death and resurrection of the Savior. (Matt. 16:28; Mark 9:1; Luke 9:27.)

9. The three Nephite disciples. (3 Nephi 28:1-40.)

10. Other individuals of whom the Lord revealed: "All are under sin, except those which I have reserved unto myself, holy men that ye know not of." (D & C 49:8.)

The translation of all the above individuals and groups of people will be discussed in greater detail in following chapters within this book.

CHAPTER 2

THE TRANSLATION OF ENOCH
AND OF THE CITY OF ENOCH

The Character and Translation of Enoch

The Bible is extremely brief in its account of the man, Enoch. All that it mentions about him is the following:

> And Jared lived after he begat Enoch eight hundred years, and begat sons and daughters:
> And all the days of Jared were nine hundred sixty and two years: and he died.
> And Enoch lived sixty and five years, and begat Methuselah:
> And Enoch walked with God after he begat Methuselah three hundred years, and begat sons and daughters;
> And all the days of Enoch were three hundred sixty and five years:
> *And Enoch walked with God: and he was not; for God took him.* (Genesis 5:19-24.)
>
> *By faith Enoch was translated that he should not see death; and was not found,* because God had translated him: for before his translation he had this testimony, that he pleased God. (Hebrews 11:5.)

However, from revealed scripture and statements made by the Prophet Joseph Smith and from comments of other modern-day Prophets and General Authorities, the character and translation of Enoch is greatly enlarged and richly portrayed. For example, the entire seventh chapter of the Book of Moses, in The Pearl of Great Price, talks about the majesty and righteousness of Enoch and of events which transpired between Enoch, the Lord, and the inhabitants of the City of

Enoch. From various chapters within the Book of Moses and comments made by the Prophet Joseph Smith and other brethren, the following facts about the life of Enoch may be outlined as follows:[1]

A. *SOME LEADING EVENTS IN THE LIFE OF ENOCH:*

1.   *His Calling to the Ministry.*—Enoch had held the Priesthood, having received it from Adam, and then at the age of sixty-five he received a special call to the ministry and was blessed by the father of the race. At about this time, too, his son, Methuselah, was leading the race in longevity.

The call of Enoch, as recorded in the Pearl of Great Price, Book of Moses 6:1-36, consisted in a series of marvelous events: (a) The Spirit of God descended out of heaven and remained on Enoch; (b) The Lord made a prophet and missionary out of Enoch; (c) God declares to Enoch the sinful condition of the people and the penalties in store for the unrepentant; (d) Enoch pleads his unpopularity among the people and his deficiency as a speaker; (e) God gives Enoch a promise of protection, and of eloquence and endows him with the power to work miracles; (f) The Lord makes Enoch a seer.

2.   *Enoch's First Missionary Work at Home.*—(a) He fearlessly denounces the wickedness of the people. (b) His sermons carried wonderment, fear, and inquiry into the hearts of the populace. (c) His invincible testimony caused the people to flee or fall before him. (d) He declared Adam's belief in Christ, his baptism, and his clear knowledge of the atonement. (e) He prophesies war and degradation in the absence of repentance. (Pearl of Great Price, Moses 7:7, 8.)

3.   *Enoch's Mission Abroad.*—(a) The Lord called him to preach to all except the conspirators with Cain. (b) He declares that baptism must be done in the name of the Father, the Son, and the Holy Ghost. (Pearl of Great Price, Moses 7:11, 12.)

---

1. *The Relief Society Magazine* (An LDS Church magazine), February, 1925, Volume 12, pp. 95-98, first printed the outline given herein.

4. *Enoch's Power in Working Miracles.*—(a) The earth trembled; mountains fled; rivers were turned out of their courses, at his command, for the protection and progress of the converts, and their enemies fled to an island. (Moses 13:15.)

5. *The Building of Zion Under Enoch's Leadership.* (Moses 7.)—(a) He established faith to the point of obedience. (b) He brought about union. (c) He kept out unrighteous living. (d) He provided industry for all under the plan of stewardships. (e) He kept out class distinction. (f) He kept in constant communion with the Lord. (g) He unceasingly provided the people with the word of the Lord, reminding them of the past, encouraging them as to the present, and revealing to them the future.

6. *The Completion and Translation of the City of Enoch.*—Enoch, the "seventh from Adam," built up a commonwealth with a perfectness akin to that of the completion of the creation. The City of Enoch, the dimensions of which are not known to us, became the abode of the Lord. Its people had been in the world but not of the world. In the midst of wickedness they were good. They were Zion, the "pure in heart." Their city became Zion, the place where God dwells.

The conditions of this unparalleled community were beyond the earth, and they were more than terrestrial. Under the law of the eternal fitness of things the city was given a position above the earth. When the Lord said of Zion, "Behold, mine abode forever," did he not indicate that the city built by men, under the direction of the Lord, was accepted as a part of his celestial kingdom? The kingdom where dwell none but those who can enjoy the personal presence of God.

The community conditions that make a Zion fit for the personal presence of the Lord are set forth in the following: "And the Lord called his people Zion, because they were of one heart and one mind, and dwelt in righteousness, and there was no poor among them." The Zion qualities of a community then, are (1) oneness of heart; (2) oneness of mind, or belief; (3) righteousness or right living; (4) community welfare or the absence of want.

These four points of consideration seem to have been the basis of the Divine judgment by which the City of Enoch was named Zion.

7.   *After the City was Translated.* Pearl of Great Price, Moses 7:23-69.—(a) He sees the extent of Satan's power on the earth and the chaining of men's minds. (b) He sees angels from heaven working to unchain men's minds. (c) He sees a side of God's nature, unthought of before. The Lord wept in his presence because of the sin-brought suffering of his wayward children. (d) He witnesses in vision the saving of Noah and his family and the replenishing of the earth. (e) He beholds the birth, life-labors, suffering, death, and triumphant resurrection of the Christ, and with him the resurrection of the Saints who had slept. (f) He hears the earth mourn because of its pollution by men. Who can say with certainty that the earth is not intelligent? At all events, it is obedient to law. (g) He obtains a promise from the Lord of this day: this day of wide spread knowledge (Moses 7:62) and a description of the meeting of the Zion above with the Zion beneath. (h) He sees the millenium and the apostacy that follows it, the final victory of the Savior and the everlasting banishment of Satan from the earth. (i) He sees done with the whole earth what he and his people have done with a part of it, made a place of which God could say, "Mine abode forever."

B. THE DOCTRINES PREACHED BY ENOCH.

1.   Those of record: free agency, faith, repentance, baptism (by water and the Spirit), resurrection, and eternal judgment.

2.   Those in evidence, but not of direct record: consecration, or stewardship responsibility.

C. BIOGRAPHICAL SUMMARY.

1.   Enoch was the "seventh from Adam."

2.   He was ordained a High Priest at the age of twenty-five by Adam.

3.   He was called to the ministry at the age of sixty-five.

4.   He preached the gospel 365 years.

5.   He proved the possibility of man's living the celestial law on a terrestrial planet.

6.   He was more than three centuries in building the Christ-ideal community.

7.   He had an intense interest in the welfare of the people of the earth after his translation.

8.   He was a prophet, seer, and revelator, with the seership seemingly predominating.

9.   He had access to God in his highest place—"Thou has given me a right to thy throne."

10.   Enoch finished the Adamic Dispensation.

The Establishment of the City of Enoch

During the time when the Prophet Enoch was upon the earth, approximately 5,000 years ago (between about 3,365 B.C. to 2,935 B.C.[1]), conditions throughout the world became so turbulent and wickedness so abundant that Enoch, under the direction of God and with the "united labors of the Elders of his day, gathered the people together who hearkened to his words" and built up a city in righteousness, which they called "Zion." Regarding this subject, President John Taylor has said the following:

Enoch was a remarkable man and had a special mission to the people in his day, and he was full of the spirit of prophecy and revelation; he also had a Church organization as we have to a certain extent, and he preached to the people and forewarned them of certain events that should transpire upon the earth. And the wicked were angry with them, as they are sometimes with us; they did not like their teachings and operations,

1. Dale A. McAllister, "An Analysis of Old Testament Chronology in the Light of Modern Scripture and Scientific Research" (Thesis, Brigham Young University, Provo, Utah, 1963), p. 119.

and they conspired against them, and great numbers of their enemies assembled for the purpose of destroying them. And Enoch was clothed upon by the power and spirit and revelation of God. And whilst under the inspiration of the Almighty he uttered his prophecies, and his enemies and the people generally trembled at the power of his words; and the earth shook, and the people fled from his presence afar off, and were not able to injure him, for God was with him. And Enoch, with the united labors of the elders of his day, gathered the people together who hearkened to his words and believed the message sent to them, in the same manner as you have been gathered together. They built up a city which was called Zion; and the people who inhabited it were under the inspiration of the Lord for a great number of years; receiving instruction, guidance and direction from him. And finally, as wickedness grew and increased, and as the testimony went forth among them, the good, the virtuous, the honorable, the pure and those who desired to fear God and work righteousness assembled themselves together, constituting the city of Zion; and the others became more corrupt. And Enoch and his brethren prophesied unto the people about the calamities that should overtake them, that the world was to be destroyed by a flood; and there were provisions made for the continuance of the human family, and it was made known to Methuselah that his seed should be the medium through which should be perpetuated the human family upon the earth. And Methuselah was so very desirous to have this thing fulfilled that Noah, his grandson, who was the son of Lamech, was ordained by Methuselah when he was ten years old.

The people, we learn, grew to be so corrupt that "the imaginations of the thoughts of their hearts were only evil, and that continually;" and we are told that it even repented the Lord that he had made man. But the servants of God went forth preaching the Gospel of life and salvation to this wicked people, and warned them of the destruction that was coming upon the earth. Before this great calamity took place, Enoch and his city were translated.[1]

President John Taylor has also stated that the inhabitants of the City of Enoch were constantly under the "guidance, direction, and teaching of the Almighty in order that they might be prepared for another Zion" in the heavens:

> In the days of Enoch...there was a remarkable work performed then according to the revelations which have been given to us, which will be more fully developed when the Lord shall see fit to reveal other things associated therewith. But we learn that there was a Church organized about as ours may be; we learn that they went forth and preached the Gospel; we learn that they were gathered together to a place called Zion; *we learn that the people of Zion were under the guidance, direction and teaching of the Almighty; in order that they might be prepared for another Zion in the grand drama associated with the dealings of God and his purposes pertaining to this earth and the heavens.* We read that they walked with God for 365 years. We are told in the Bible a little short story about it, because it was one of those things that it was not necessary that everybody should know.[2]

As to the specific nature and activity, yesterday and today, of the inhabitants of the City of Enoch, Elder George W. Crocheron has written rather comprehensively and eloquently the following description:

> President Brigham Young said, in a sermon delivered June 3, 1860, "Enoch was the only man that could build a city to God; and as soon as he had it completed, he and his city, with all its walls, houses, lands, rivers, and everything pertaining to it, were taken away."

---

1. John Taylor, *Journal of Discourses*, Volume 21, pp. 242-243.
2. *Ibid.*, Volume 26, p. 34.

The scriptures inform us that Enoch walked and talked with God three hundred and sixty-five years. We have no biblical data upon which to form a correct idea of the population inhabiting that truly wonderful city, but the inference would justify the belief that the population must have been of an exceeding great number. Doubtless they were, to a great extent, an agriculture people, embracing the cultivation of cereals, grasses and fruits. The manufacture of various fabrics of clothing and the handiwork created by skilled labor, incidental to various trades, were among the necessities required for the community. That there were poets, philosophers, historians, artists, inventors and men and women possessing genius of various grades, the writer does not doubt.

We may believe they were a self-sustaining community, since history, either sacred or profane, does not treat of interchange of their products with other nationalities. Therefore, strictly speaking, a marked exclusiveness was maintained among them. They were bound together in the indissoluble bonds of love and fraternity, in the most exalted sense of those terms. Speculation in values, the desire to hoard up wealth for self-aggrandizement, which fosters the spirit of pride, had no place among them. Their lives and environments presented a picture of millennial bliss, and in a certain degree, it may be called the first millennium on earth, because the powers of darkness held no dominion over them, so great was their union. So universal was the spirit of love enjoyed by Enoch's people that it would seem that the animal creation and the birds of the air must have partaken of the divine influence prevailing, while marked results were witnessed in the increase of the earth's products of grains and fruits.

What was the primal cause which brought about this happy condition of society, socially, religiously and industrially? It was due to the people having consecrated their time, talents, and all their earthly possessions, to one common end—the good of the whole

community. The words of the Master will find applica-
tion here, "Except ye are one, ye are not mine." The
people of Enoch were a unit in keeping the law of consecration, hence the blessings which followed. We are
told that when conditions become favorable, in a future
day, the glorious principle of consecration will again be
introduced as a preparatory event preceding the coming of the Lord. Who will abide this great law of exaltation? Those whose eyes are single to the glory of God
and to the upbuilding of his great latter-day work, for
the glory of Zion, "and the perfecting of the Saints."

The principle of consecration was alluded to, in a
limited sense, when the Savior said to the rich young
man, "Go and sell that thou hast, and give it to the
poor, and thou shalt have treasure in heaven: and come
and follow me." We are told that we shall be tried in all
things. Some persons have apostatized from the church
because of poverty, others from having gained great
wealth; so, we see that these two extremes have wrecked
the salvation of certain individuals. It is said that the
optic nerve is one of the most sensitive in the human
being. Some persons who possess a very strong feeling
of holding on to property, are like the rich young man
whom the Savior conversed with, and these will doubtless refuse to accept the law of consecration. Hence,
the need of these words of admonition: if prosperity
floweth unto thee like a river, be humble, keep the
faith. Should poverty assail you, in its most threaten-
ing form: be humble, keep the faith. Let the spiritual
have precedence, hold the temporal in abeyance. When
this order of procedure is reversed, a person is tres-
passing on dangerous ground.

Referring to the extract from President Young's
sermon, what a wonderful exhibition of the power of
the Almighty was witnessed when Enoch's city was
translated! Hail to the day of its return to earth, when
the earth is prepared for its reception![1]

---

1. *The Improvement Era* (an LDS Church magazine), April, 1905,
Volume 8, pp. 536-538.

The Translation of the City of Enoch

The Prophet Joseph Smith has told us that Enoch and all the inhabitants in the City of Enoch attained in their day unto a terrestrial glory, a glory they still enjoy.[1] Because of this terrestrial state of glory, which they attained to through their righteousness and knowledge while still upon the earth, they were eventually translated, taking their bodies and their city with them to "some part or portion of space" reserved for them.[2]

In 1874, Elder Orson Pratt elaborated on the translation of the inhabitants of the City of Enoch, mentioning when and why they were translated and their present activity and future destiny in regards to the ministry of the gospel to individuals of a terrestrial order. He said:

> How much of the earth was taken up in connection with their habitations we are not informed. It might have been a large region. You may ask—*"Where was this city of Zion built in ancient days?" According to new revelation it was built upon this great western hemisphere.* When I speak of this western hemisphere I speak of it as it now exists. *In those days the land was united; the eastern and the western hemispheres were one;* but they dwelt in that portion of our globe that is now called the western hemisphere, and they were taken up from this portion of the globe. *No doubt all the region of country occupied by them was translated, or taken away from the earth.*
>
> Does this prove that they were immortal beings from the time of their translation? No; it does not prove any such thing. How are we to know anything about it? We can not learn anything in relation to it, except by revelation. *God has revealed to us that they are held in reserve, in some part or portion of space; their location is not revealed,* but they are held in

---

1. Franklin D. Richards, *Journal of Discourses,* Volume 25, p. 236.
2. Orson Pratt, *Journal of Discourses,* Volume 17, p. 147.

reserve to be revealed in the latter times, to return to their ancient mother earth; all the inhabitants that were then taken away are to return to the earth.

Some five thousand years have passed away since they were caught up to the heavens. What has been their condition during that time? Have they been free from death? They have been held in reserve in answer to their prayers. What were their prayers? Enoch and his people prayed that a day of righteousness might be brought about during their day; they sought for it with all their hearts; they looked abroad over the face of the earth and saw the corruptions that had been introduced by the nations, the decendants of Adam, and their hearts melted within them, and they groaned before the Lord with pain and sorrow, because of the wickedness of the children of men, and they sought for a day of rest, they sought that righteousness might be revealed, that wickedness might be swept away and that the earth might rest for a season. God gave them visions, portrayed to them the future of the world, showed unto them that this earth must fulfill the measure of its creation; that generation after generation must be born and pass away, and that, after a certain period of time, the earth would rest from wickedness, that the wicked would be swept away, and the earth would be cleansed and sanctified and be prepared for a righteous people. "Until that day," saith the Lord, "you and your people shall rest, Zion shall be taken up into my own bosom." Ancient Zion should be held in reserve until the day of rest should come, "then," said the Lord to Enoch, "thou and all thy city shall descend upon the earth, and your prayers shall be answered."

They have been gone, as I have already stated, about five thousand years. What have they been doing? All that we know concerning this subject is what has been revealed through the great and mighty Prophet of the last days, Joseph Smith—that unlearned youth whom God raised up to bring forth the Book of Mormon and to establish this latter-day Church. He has told us that *they have been ministering angels during all that time. To whom? To those of the terrestrial order*, if you can understand that expression. God gave them the desires of their hearts, the same as he gave to the three Nephites, to whom he gave the privilege, according to their request of remaining and bringing souls unto Christ while the world should stand. Even so, *he granted to the people of Enoch their desire to become ministering spirits unto those of the terrestrial order until the earth should rest and they should again return to it....*

Strangers will not understand perhaps what we mean by the terrestrial order. If they will take the opportunity of reading the doctrines of this Church, as laid down in the revelations given through Joseph Smith, they will learn what our views are in relation to this matter. God revealed by vision the different orders of being in the eternal worlds. One class, the highest of all, is called the celestial; another class, the next to the celestial in glory, power, might and dominion, is called the terrestrial; another class, still lower than the terrestrial in glory and exaltation, is called the telestial. *This middle class, whose glory is typified by the glory of our moon in the firmament of the heavens as compared with the sun, are those who once dwelt on this or some other creation and, if they have had the Gospel laid before them they have not had a full opportunity of receiving it; or they have not heard it all, and have died without having the privilege. In the resurrection they come forth with terrestrial bodies. They must be administered to says the vision, and God has appointed agents or messengers to minister to these terrestrial beings, for their good, blessing, exaltation, glory and honor in the eternal worlds.*

Enoch and his people understanding this principle sought that they, before receiving the fullness of their celestial glory, might be the instruments in the hands of God of doing much good among beings of the terrestrial order.

We read in the New Testament concerning certain angels that are in the eternal worlds, and the question is asked by the Apostle Paul—"Are they not all ministering spirits, sent forth to minister for those who shall be heirs of salvation?"—not for those who were already heirs of salvation, but for those who *shall* be— those who were to be redeemed, that were to be brought forth and exalted. *Enoch and his people were appointed to this ministry, holding the Priesthood thereof, with power and authority to administer in order that those beings may be exalted and brought up, and inherit all the glory that they are desirous to receive.*[1]

In addition, one should remember that all those people who were translated before the resurrection of our Lord, which includes Enoch and the inhabitants of his city, "were with Christ in his resurrection." (D & C 133:55.) Therefore, it will be resurrected, not translated beings, who shall return with the city of Enoch to the earth in the last days.

---

1. *Ibid.*, pp. 147-149.

CHAPTER 3

THE TRANSLATION OF JOHN THE REVELATOR

A Biographical Sketch of John the Revelator

John the Revelator, also called John the Beloved, was the closest to the Lord of all the Twelve Apostles during the Savior's mortal ministry in the meridian of time. He is known through scripture as "the disciple whom Jesus loved" (John 13:23.) and "prized this appellation," using it "more often than any other" introduction "when referring to himself" in writing. Like the three Nephites, John the Revelator chose to be translated and to remain upon the earth, thereby making his mission upon the earth longer so that he would be able to "postpone the day of his exaltation, that he might perchance save someone who might otherwise be lost."[1] From scripture and secular sources a brief biographical sketch of John the Revelator may be presented as follows:

JOHN THE REVELATOR[2]

He was a cousin of Jesus according to the flesh, from his mother, a sister of Mary. This relationship, together with the enthusiasm of youth and the fervor of his emotional nature, formed the basis of his intimacy with the Lord.

John was a son, probably the younger son, of Zebedee and Salome and a brother of the elder James who became the pro-martyr of the apostles.

The name given him by his parents expressed the thought "Jehovah is gracious" indicative of his gentle, lovable disposition. The title meaning "Son of Thunder" given him by the

---

1. *The Relief Society Magazine, op. cit.*, December, 1926, Volume 13, pp. 635-637.
2. *Ibid.*

Savior is representative of his fearlessness in defending the truth and denouncing unrighteousness.

Note the manifestation of the two phases of greatness in the following:

There is no fear in love; but perfect love casteth out fear; because fear hath torment. He that feareth, is not made perfect in love.

We love him, because he first loved us.

If a man say, I love God, and hateth his brother whom he hath seen, how can he love God whom he hath not seen?

And this commandment have we from him, That he who loveth God love his brother also. (I John, 4:18-21.)

Observe how frequently he uses the expression "beloved" in his letters to the Saints. (See I John 3-4.)

Christian art has so far well understood the double aspect of John by representing him with a face of womanly purity and tenderness, but not weakness, and giving him for his symbol a bold eagle soaring with outspread wings above the clouds. (Schaff's *History of the Christian Church*, Vol. I, p. 419.)

His second epistle, a letter to an "elect lady," is typical of his pastoral care.

John's vocation was that of his father, a prosperous fisherman. He, no doubt, had a home in Galilee or Jerusalem to which he took and cared for the mother of Jesus. He became a disciple of John the Baptist, and following the testimony of the latter became a follower of Jesus.

As a member of the Twelve *he was one of three with whom the Savior most often counseled*, and of these three John seems to have kept closest to the Savior, and *was known as the "disciple whom the Lord loved."* He prized this apellation and used it more often than any other when referring to himself.

John's interest in the mission of Christ: The proving of his undying love for others, and the winning of the lasting love of others, were most self-denying. John, the closest of all to Christ, chose to make his mission longer...to extend the period of absence from his beloved Leader, and to postpone the day of his exaltation, that he might perchance save someone who might otherwise be lost.

Tradition says, "When in his old age on a tour of visitation, he lovingly pursued one of his former converts who had become a robber, and reclaimed him to the Church."

And the Lord said unto me: John, my beloved, what desirest thou? For if ye shall ask what you will, it shall be granted unto you.

And I said unto him: Lord, give unto me power over death, that I may live and bring souls unto thee.

And the Lord said unto me: Verily, verily, I say unto thee, *because thou desirest this thou shalt tarry until I come in my glory, and shalt prophesy before nations, kindred, tongues and people.*

And for this cause the Lord said unto Peter, If I will that he tarry till I come, what is that to thee? For he desired of me that he might bring souls unto me, but thou desiredst that thou mightest speedily come unto me in my kingdom.

I say unto thee, Peter, this was a good desire; but *my beloved has desired that he might do more, or a greater work yet among men than what he has before done.*

Yea, he has undertaken a greater work; therefore I will make him as flaming fire and a ministering angel; he shall minister for those who shall be heirs of salvation who dwell on the earth.

And I will make thee to minister for him and for thy brother James; and unto you three I will give this power and the keys of this ministry until I come.

Verily, I say unto you, ye shall both have according to your desires, for ye both joy in that which ye have desired. (D & C, sec. 7.)

John was the only apostle of record at the tragedy of Calvary. He was the last person to receive a commission from the Master in mortality. He was the first man at the sepulcher of the resurrected Christ and the first to recognize the Redeemer at the seashore.

With the promise of being permitted to remain on earth until the second coming of Christ, John so powerfully pushed the work of the Master that he became the special object of pagan hate and persecution. Failing in their attempts to take his life they struck at his liberty, and banished him to the Isle of Patmos, a place of desolation and loneliness in the Aegean Sea, southwest from Ephesus. [He remained on the island until about 96 A.D.]

His contributions to scripture, though not voluminous, are of high value. The Fourth Gospel has been called the best by capable critics. The epistles of John have been given high place by scriptorians, and the Book of Revelations, with its historical reach extending back of earth-life, and its prophetic illumination shining beyond the millennium, is still waiting for interpretation.

The Visions and Translation of John the Revelator

Elder Orson F. Whitney has stated that before John the Revelator was translated, "God condescended to reveal to (John) what should come to pass in the last days" and that the Book of Revelation "is a record which the Apostle left of the great things that were shown him, and which he should remain upon the earth to see." Also, "not only was John shown what should occur after the time in which he was living, but he was shown what had already taken place," for "the events of the seven thousand years of the world's temporal existence passed before him, like the scenes of a mighty panorama."[1] Concerning the magnitude and significance of the visions and of the translation which John the Revelator received during his apostolic ministry in the old world, Elder Whitney has further said:

> The Latter-day Saints are taught that Jesus, on a certain occasion, speaking to the Twelve, wished to bestow upon them each a gift, to grant the desire of their hearts, and He asked them what they would He should do for them. They all but one requested to be taken

---

1. Orson F. Whitney, *Journal of Discourses*, Volume 26, pp. 263-264.

home to Him in heaven when they should have filled
the allotted age of man. But one turned away sorrow-
ful, feeling that the wish he cherished in his heart was
too great to be granted. Peter asked the Savior, "What
shall this man do?" and received the reply, "If I will
that he tarry till I come what is that to thee?" "Then
went this saying abroad among the brethren that that
disciple should not die." It is vaguely given, I admit, in
the Bible from which I have quoted, but modern revelation has made it plainer, and shown us that the *Apostle
John obtained a promise from the Savior that he should
remain upon the earth to witness the downfall and the
rise of nations, that he should live to perform a mighty
mission in the midst of the children of men; that he
should prophesy before kings and rulers, and should
tarry upon the earth until the Son of God came in His
glory.* This Apostle was the only one who escaped the
tragic fate of his fellows. He was the only one of the
original Twelve who was not put to death. An attempt
was made upon his life by throwing him into a cauldron
of boiling oil, but he escaped miraculously, and his
enemies, not having the power to put him to death,
banished him to the desert island of Patmos. It was
during his exile upon this lonely spot, that *God condescended to reveal to him what should come to pass
in the last days,* and the book which is called the
Apocalypse is a record which the Apostle left of the
great things that were shown him, and which he should
remain upon the earth to see. An angel appeared unto
him, John mistook him, it seems, for the Lord, and
fell down at his feet to worship him, his person was so
glorious. But the angel reproved him and said, "See
thou do it not: for I am thy fellow-servant and of thy
brethren the prophets." Here was one of the prophets
who had been slain for the testimony of Jesus, who was
so glorious when he appeared that John, who perhaps
had labored with him, did not recognize him. He had
been sent unto him to show him what should come to
pass thereafter.

But not only was John shown what should occur after the time in which he was living, but he was shown what had already taken place; not as the imperfect records of profane history have given it to us, but he saw it typified in its fullness. *The events of the seven thousand years of the world's temporal existence passed before him, like the scenes of a mighty panorama.* If you will read the book which he left, you will there find portrayed symbolically each of the seven thousand years. He saw the events which had followed the creation down until one period had passed; he then saw the events of the second thousand years or until two periods had passed, and then the third and the fourth periods, at the end of which Jesus came as the Savior of mankind, to perform a personal work in the flesh, John saw, further, the events of the fifth thousand years. He saw the great apostacy that was to take place in the Christian church, when they put to death every inspired man; when they did away with the gifts and blessings of the Holy Ghost; when they said they were no longer necessary; when they engrafted upon the olive tree of the Christian faith the wild branches of paganism. He saw all this taking place down to the sixth thousand years, and after the world had wandered in darkness for centuries, he says

"And I saw another angel fly in the midst of heaven, having the everlasting Gospel to preach unto them that dwell on the earth, and to every nation and kindred, and tongue, and people.

"Saying with a loud voice, fear God, and give glory to Him; for the hour of His judgment is come; and worship Him that made heaven, and earth, and the sea, and the fountains of waters."

Showing conclusively, as well as language can show, that this was to be an event of the last days— the hour of God's judgment, which Christianity itself, in its perverted state, will admit is at the end of the world. John saw the angel restoring the Gospel shortly before the hour of God's judgment, saying with a loud voice to all nations, kindreds, tongues and peoples—not only to the heathen nations, but to those who professed to have the true Christian faith—"Fear God, and give glory to Him, for the hour of his judgment is come." This to us is another proof of the apostasy of the Christian world; for if they had the truth, as they claim, by apostolic succession, from St. Peter down to the present day—what need of restoring the Gospel in its fullness to preach to them? It would be superfluous, unnecessary, a work of supererogation, to preach to those who were living in the full blaze of Gospel light, and call upon them to repent of their sins.[1]

In addition it also appears that today as a translated being John the Revelator not only acts presently as one of the Lord's ministering angels unto "all nations, kindred, tongues and people" upon this earth,[2] but likewise serves as a special messenger of the Lord to the lost Ten Tribes of the "northern countries;" for Elder Franklin D. Richards has said:

When Enoch and his people come back, they will come back with their city, their temples, blessings and powers. The north country will yield up its multitude (of the Ten Tribes), *with the Apostle John, who is looking after them.* They also will come to Zion and receive their crowns at the hands of their brethren of Ephraim.[3]

---

1. *Ibid.*
2. *The Relief Society Magazine, op. cit.*, December, 1926, Volume 13, p. 636.
3. Franklin D. Richards, *Journal of Discourses*, Volume 25, p. 237.

CHAPTER 4

THE TRANSLATION OF THE THREE NEPHITES

The Translation, Purposes, and Prophesies of the Three Nephites

The translation of the "Three Nephites," who were three of the original twelve Nephite disciples whom the Lord had chosen after He had established His Church upon the American continent, is explained in more scriptural detail than any other recorded translation. In one of the greatest discourses on the translation, purposes, and prophesies of the Three Nephites, Elder Orson Pratt, on Sunday, April 11, 1875, in the Salt Lake Tabernacle, delivered from scriptural sources the following inspirational sermon on the Three Nephites:

Since God brought forth this sign, the Book of Mormon...he has begun to work among the remnants of the house of Israel, the American Indians, upon this continent, by his own power. What is it that has stirred them up to believe in this work? Has it been your exertion? Not altogether; yet, no doubt, you, in some small degree, as far as your faith would permit, have helped on the work among these wild tribes. You have sought to recover them, you have fed and clothed them to some extent; you have told them occasionally about the records of their fathers; you have tried to bring them to repentance; but after years of labor, you have said—"Alas! alas for them: What can be done to reclaim a people so far fallen into the depths of ignorance and corruption?" Your hearts have been almost discouraged so far as your own labors were concerned. But how soon and how marvelously, when the time had come, has the Lord our God begun to operate upon them as nations and as tribes, bringing them in from hundreds

of miles distant to inquire after the Elders of this
Church. What for? What do they want with the Elders?
They want to be baptized. Who told them to come and
be baptized? *They say that men came to them in their
dreams, and spoke to them in their own language, and
told them that away yonder was a people who had
authority from God to baptize them; but that they
must repent of their sins, cease their evil habits and lay
aside the traditions of their fathers, for they were false;
that they must cease to roam over the face of the land,
robbing and plundering, and learn to live as the white
people.*

Who are these men who have been to the Indians
and told them to repent of their sins, and be baptized
by the "Mormons?" *They are men who obtained the
promise of the Lord, upwards of eighteen centuries
ago, that they should be instruments in his hands of
bringing about the redemption of their descendants.
The Lord God promised them the privilege of working
for and in behalf of their descendants in the latter
days; and they have begun the work.* All this was fore-
told in this record, the Book of Mormon.

Now I will read a little for the benefit of the
Latter-day Saints [from 3 Nephi 28:1-40 and Mormon
8:10-11, in the Book of Mormon], for though they
have this record lying upon their shelves, I fear there
are some who are careless about reading its contents,
and perhaps do not understand the signs of the times,
and the fulfillment of the purposes of God, which are
here so clearly set forth. Jesus appeared on this
American Continent soon after his resurrection, three
different times that are recorded, and how many other
times that are not recorded, I do not know. But he
showed himself to them and brake bread with them.
But the third time he came to the Twelve whom he had
chosen on this land,—as he was about to leave them
he put a very important question to them. He said unto his twelve disciples, speaking unto them one by

one—"What is it that you desire of me, after that I am gone unto the Father?" And they all spake save it were three—"We desire that, after we have lived unto the age of men, that our ministry wherein thou hast called us may have an end, and that we may speedily come to thee in thy kingdom." And he said unto them—"Blessed are ye because ye have desired this thing of me; therefore after that ye are seventy-two years old, ye shall come unto me in my kingdom, and with me ye shall find rest." And when he had spoken these words unto the nine, he then turns to the three and said unto them— "What will ye that I shall do unto you when I am gone to the Father?" And they sorrowed in their hearts, for they dare not speak unto him the thing which they desired. And he said unto them—"*Behold, I know your thoughts, and you have desired the thing which John, my beloved, who was with me in my ministry before I was lifted up by the Jews, desired of me, therefore more blessed are ye, for ye shall never taste of death.*" These three men had the promise that they should never taste death; "but," said the Savior unto them—"*ye shall live to behold all the doings of the Father unto the children of men, even until all things shall be fulfilled according to the will of the Father, when I come in my glory with the powers of heaven. Ye shall never endure the pains of death, but when I shall come in my glory, ye shall be changed in the twinkling of an eye from mortality to immortality; then shall ye be blessed in the kingdom of my Father. And again ye shall not have pain while ye shall dwell in the flesh, neither sorrow,* save it be for the sins of the world; and all this will I do because of the thing which ye have desired of me; for *ye have desired that ye may bring the souls of men unto me while the world shall stand; and for this cause ye shall have fulness of joy,* and ye shall sit down in the kingdom of my Father; yea your joy shall be full, even as the Father hath given me fulness of joy; and ye shall be even as I am, and I am even as the Father, and the Father and I are one; and the Holy Ghost beareth record of the Father and me; and the Father giveth the Holy Ghost unto the children of men because of me."

What a glorious promise was made to these three men! Did they receive any change? Yes, they did; not to immortality however, but *a change sufficient was wrought in their bodies that death should not have power over them.* But let us read a little further, it is very interesting. "And it came to pass that when Jesus had spoken these words, he touched every one of them with his finger save it were the three who were to tarry;" that is, he touched the nine who were to preach until they were seventy-two years old and who were then to be taken home to God, "and then he departed, and behold the heavens were opened and *they (the three) were caught up into heaven, and saw and heard unspeakable things.* And it was forbidden them that they should utter; neither was it given unto them power that they could utter the things which they saw and heard; and *whether they were in the body or out of the body they could not tell,* for it did seem unto them like a transfiguration of things." That is the way that they received their partial change. "But it came to pass that they did again minister upon the face of the earth; nevertheless they did not minister of the things which they had heard and seen, because of the commandment which was given them in heaven."

Now these men lived in the first century of the Christian era on this continent; and when that generation all passed away they also lived in the second century of the Christian era, and ministered to the ancient inhabitants on this land. And when the second century had all passed off the stage of action they also lived in the third century; and in the fourth century *the Lord took these three men from the midst of the remnant of Israel on this land.* Where did he take them? I do not know, it is not revealed. Why did he take them away? Because of the apostacy of the people, because the people were unworthy of the ministration of such great and holy men; because they sought to kill them; because they cast them into dens of wild beasts twice; and these men of God played with these wild beasts as a child would play with a suckling lamb, and received no harm from them. They cast them three times into a furnace of fire, and they came forth therefrom and received no hurt. They dug deep pits in the earth and cast them therein, supposing that they would perish; but by the power of the word of God that was in them, they smote the earth in the name of the Lord, and were delivered from these pits. And thus they went forth performing signs, wonders and miracles among this remnant of Israel, until their wickedness became so great that the Lord commanded them to depart out of their midst. And the remnant of Israel, from that day to the present—between fourteen and fifteen centuries— have been dwindling in unbelief, in ignorance, and in all the darkness which now surrounds them; but notwithstanding their darkness and misery, the three Nephites, for many generations, have not administered to them, because of the commandment of the Almighty to them.

But are they always to remain silent? Are there no more manifestations to come from these three men? Are they never again to remember the remnants of the House of Israel on this land? Let us read the promise. "Behold I was about to write the names of those who were never to taste of death, but the Lord forbade; therefore I write them not, for they are hid from the world; but behold I have seen them." Mormon saw them nearly four centuries after they were caught up into heaven, and after they received their partial change. Mormon saw them and they administered unto him. He says—"Behold I have seen them and they have ministered unto me; and behold *they will be among the Gentiles, and the Gentiles knoweth them not.*" They will, no doubt, call them poor deluded Mormons, and say that they ought to be hooted out of society, and they ought to be persecuted, afflicted, and hated by all people. "They will be among the Gentiles and the

Gentiles knoweth them not. *They will also be among the Jews, and the Jews shall know them not.* And it shall come to pass when the Lord seeth fit, in his wisdom, that *they shall minister unto all the scattered tribes of Israel, and unto all nations, kindreds, tongues and people, and shall bring out of them unto Jesus many souls,* that their desire may be fulfilled; and also because of the convincing power of God which is in them; and *they are as the angels of God.* And if they shall pray unto the Father in the name of Jesus, *they can show themselves unto whatsoever man it seemeth them good;* therefore great and marvelous works shall be wrought by them before the great and coming day when all people must surely stand before the judgment seat of Christ. Yea even among the Gentiles shall there be a great and a marvelous work wrought by them, before that judgment day."

Now, having read these things, *let us come back again to this spiritual movement that we hear of among the remnants of Jacob, in these western deserts, in the northwest hundreds of miles, in the west and in the southwest. It is not confined to hundreds, but thousands testify that men have appeared individually in dreams, speaking their own language* and, as Brother Hyde said last Tuesday, *these men tell their descendants what their duties are, what they should do, and how they should hunt up this people, repent of their sins, be baptized, etc.* And the parties who have been thus instructed time and time again, have fulfilled the commandments that they received, and some of them have come hundreds of miles to be baptized, and they are now desirous of laying aside their savage disposition, their roaming habits, and they want to learn to cultivate the earth, to lay down their weapons of war, cease stealing and to become a peaceable good people.[1]

On another occasion Elder Orson Pratt also explained why the Three Nephites do not "lift up their voices in

---

1. Orson Pratt, *Journal of Discourses*, Volume 18, pp. 18-23.

the midst of our congregations," to publicly announce their presence upon the earth:

> Do you suppose that these three Nephites have any knowledge of what is going on in this land [of America]? *They know all about it; they are filled with the spirit of prophecy.* Why do they not come into our midst? Because the time has not come. Why do they not lift up their voices in the midst of our congregation? Because there is a work for us to do preparatory to their reception, and when that is accomplished, they will accomplish their work, unto whomsoever they desire to minister.[1]

In addition, Elder Franklin D. Richards has said that the actual translation of the Three Nephites was "probably" accomplished under the direction of the Savior "in one of Enoch's temples:"

> The three Nephites...wanted to tarry until Jesus came, and that they might *He took them into the heavens and endowed them with the power of translation, probably in one of Enoch's temples,* and brought them back to the earth. Thus they received power to live until the coming of the Son of Man. *I believe He took them to Enoch's city and gave them their endowments there. I expect that in the city of Enoch there are temples;* and when Enoch and his people come back, they will come back with their city, their temples, blessings and powers.[2]

The Ministry of the Three Nephites Today

Elder John W. Taylor has expressed that today the Three Nephites, as translated beings, "are going abroad in the

1. *Ibid.*, Volume 2, p. 264.
2. Franklin D. Richards, *Journal of Discourses*, Volume 25, pp. 236-237.

nations of the earth...preparing the hearts of the children of men to receive the Gospel." His statement is as follows:

> A portion of Israel is now gathered together, but in a little while you will find another prophecy will be fulfilled, and that is the prophecy that Jesus made to the three Nephites who, having power over death, are still living upon this continent. *He spoke to them of a time when they would perform a great and mighty work among the Gentiles; and that has not yet been fulfilled, but it will be. You will find that many districts where the Elders of Israel cannot reach will be penetrated by these men who have power over death;* and when the honest in heart see the power and authority that is with them, they will feel like Nicodemus did of old (but I trust they will have more faith and courage) when he said, "Rabbi, we know that thou art a teacher come from God: for no man can do these miracles that thou doest, except God be with him." These three men are going to perform a great work in the program of the last days, as is the beloved disciple John [the Revelator]....
>
> My testimony is that *these men are going abroad in the nations of the earth before the face of your sons, and they are preparing the hearts of the children of men to receive the Gospel.* They are administering to those who are heirs of salvation, and preparing their hearts to receive the truth, just as the farmer prepares the soil to receive the seed. The Lord has promised that He would send His angels before the face of His servants, and He does so.[1]

Likewise, Elder George Q. Cannon has added that the Three Nephites are serving today as "agents in the hands of God" in bringing to pass in these last days the spread of the Gospel throughout the world:

---

1. John W. Taylor, *Conference Report* (of the LDS Church), October 6, 1902, p. 75.

I have had my thoughts attracted, in consequence of a visit which brother Brigham, jun., and myself made to the hill Cumorah about three weeks ago, to the three Nephites who have been upon this land, and I have been greatly comforted at reading the promises of God concerning their labors and the work that should be accomplished by them among the Gentiles and among the Jews, also before the coming of the Lord Jesus. *I doubt not that they are laboring today in the great cause on the earth. There are agencies laboring for the accomplishment of the purposes of God and for the fulfillment of the predictions of the holy Prophets, of which we have but little conception at the present time.* We are engrossed by our own labors.... There are powers engaged in preparing the earth for the events that await it and fulfilling all the great predictions concerning it, which we know nothing of, and *we need not think that it depends upon us Latter-day Saints alone,* and that we are the only agents in the hands of God in bringing these things to pass. The powers of heaven are engaged with us in this work.[1]

---

1. George Q. Cannon, *Journal of Discourses,* Volume 16, pp. 120-121.

CHAPTER 5

OTHERS WHO HAVE BEEN TRANSLATED

Saints Between the Time of Enoch and Melchizedek Were Translated

During the nearly 700 years from the time of Enoch's translation to the flood of Noah, it appears that nearly all of the faithful members of the Church were translated, for "the Holy Ghost fell on many" during that time "and they were caught up by the powers of heaven into Zion [the translated City of Enoch]." (Moses 7:27.)

After the flood during the time of Noah and among the people of Melchizedek, the process of translation was still going on. Concerning this period of time, the *Inspired Version* of the Bible gives the following account:

> *And men having this faith, coming up unto this order of God, were translated and taken up into heaven.*
>
> And now, Melchizedek was a priest of this order; therefore he obtained peace in Salem, and was called the Prince of Peace.
>
> *And his people wrought righteousness, and obtained heaven, and sought for the city of Enoch which God had before taken, separating it from the earth,* having reserved it unto the latter days, or the end of the world." (Inspired Version, Genesis 14:32-34.)

All these people were resurrected at the time of the Savior's resurrection. (See D & C 133:53-55.)

Moses

In the Old Testament the account that Moses died and was buried by the hand of the Lord in an unknown grave is an error, for latter-day scripture indicates that Moses was translated. If, however, the expression "buried by the hand of the Lord" is a figure of speech used to indicate that the Lord translated Moses, then the statement would be correct, for in Alma 45:19 in the *Book of Mormon*, we read that the Prophet Alma was "taken up by the Spirit, or buried by the hand of the Lord, *even as Moses. But behold, the scriptures saith the Lord took Moses unto himself.*"

In addition, it is believed that Moses and the Prophet Elijah were translated so that they could come to the earth with bodies of flesh and bones to confer keys upon Peter, James, and John on the Mount of Transfiguration, an event which had to occur prior to the resurrection of the Savior. (Matt. 17:1-6.)[1] Moses was resurrected at the time of the Savior's resurrection. (See D & C 133:53-55.)

Elijah

In the Old Testament, the account of Elijah being taken in "a chariot of fire...by a whirlwind into heaven" is a majestic account of his translation. (2 Kings 2:11.) Concerning Elijah's translation, President Joseph Fielding Smith has written:

> There is a prevailing notion in the world that Elijah was taken into heaven without passing through mortal death. This could not be before the resurrection of Jesus, who became the "first fruits of the resurrection." *Elijah was a translated person, just like John the Revelator and the three Nephites.*[2]

Elijah was resurrected at the time of the Savior's resurrection. (See D & C 133:53-55.)

---

1. Bruce R. McConkie, *Doctrines of Salvation: Sermons and Writings of Joseph Fielding Smith* (Bookcraft, Inc., Salt Lake City, Utah, 1954), Volume 2, pp. 107-111.

Bruce R. McConkie, *Mormon Doctrine, op. cit.*, pp. 804-805.

Joseph Fielding Smith, *Teachings of the Prophet Joseph Smith* (Deseret News Press, Salt Lake City, Utah, 1938), p. 158.

2. Joseph Fielding Smith, *Answers..., op. cit.*, Volume 3, pp. 92-93.

Alma the Younger

Alma the Younger was translated in a similar manner to Moses. This becomes apparent when we read the following account of Alma's translation in Alma 45:18-19 in the *Book of Mormon:*

> And when Alma had done this he departed out of the land of Zarahemla, as if to go into the land of Melek. And it came to pass that *he was never heard of more; as to his death or burial we know not of.*
>
> Behold, this we know, that he was a righteous man; and the saying went abroad in the church that *he was taken up by the Spirit, or buried by the hand of the Lord, even as Moses. But behold, the scriptures saith the Lord took Moses unto himself; and we suppose that he has also received Alma in the spirit, unto himself; therefore, for this cause we know nothing concerning his death and burial.*

Alma, like Moses, was also resurrected at the time of the Savior's resurrection. (See D & C 133:53-55.)

Nephi, the Son of Helaman

It is possible that Nephi, the son of Helaman, was translated. In 3 Nephi 1:3, in the *Book of Mormon* we read the following:

> Then he [Nephi] departed out of the land, and whither he went, no man knoweth; and his son Nephi did keep the records in his stead, yea, the record of this people.

Some Latter-day Saint writers have stated that this scripture would seem to indicate the translation of Nephi, since a similar scripture is found in Alma 45:18 which mentions the translation of Alma and Elijah.[1] If Nephi was translated, he

---

1. Example: Duane S. Crowther, *op. cit.,* p. 123.

would have been resurrected at the time of the Savior's resurrection. (See D & C 133:53-55.)

Some Saints Translated During the Early Christian Era

From the following scriptures it appears that some saints who were living in the Old World following the death and resurrection of the Savior might have been translated. If they were, then they are still upon the earth or elsewhere in a translated state:

> Verily I say unto you, *There be some standing here, which shall not taste of death, till they see the Son of man coming in his kingdom.* (Matt. 16:28.)

> And he said unto them, Verily I say unto you, That *there be some of them that stand here, which shall not taste of death, till they have seen the kingdom of God come with power.* (Mark 9:1; see also Luke 9:27.)

Other Individuals Who Were Translated

Additional individuals, and/or groups of people, apparently have been translated and are still upon the earth or elsewhere in a translated nature; for the Lord has said:

> Wherefore, I will that all men shall repent, for all are under sin, except *those which I have reserved unto myself, holy men that ye know not of.* (D & C 49:8.)

CHAPTER 6

MODERN ACCOUNTS OF THE VISITATIONS
OF JOHN THE REVELATOR AND THE THREE NEPHITES

As mentioned in chapters three and four of this book, John the Revelator and the Three Nephites are still upon this earth in a translated form, and are presently serving as "ministering angels" of the Lord "unto all nations, kindred, tongues, and people" to bring mankind unto a knowledge of the Savior and of His gospel.[1] Because these translated brethren minister unto the inhabitants of the earth, it is not unusual to learn that they are fulfilling their missions upon this planet by appearing to individuals to whom the Lord has designated they should visit.

However, like any testimonial or story which deals with spiritual manifestations, through time and the passing of information from one person to another, specific accounts of such visitations, like those by John the Revelator and the Three Nephites, often become altered, questionable, or altogether lost. It is for this reason that President Joseph Fielding Smith has written the following about determining the validity of such stories dealing with translated beings:

As to the meaning of my remark: "unless the story can be properly authenticated," in reference to purported visitations of the three Nephites, all I can say is that *we should take into consideration the character and creditability of the witness, based upon his previous life.* I know of no rule that can be laid down, but when a story comes to me of this kind and I discover flaws in it, or what appear to be flaws, I reject it, and if there is evidence to support it, as we discover in the story told by David Whitmer about the preparation of his field in the night, which enabled him to make his jour-

---

1. *The Book of Mormon*, 3 Nephi 28:29.

ney to meet the Prophet, we have some tangible evidence. *There are individuals with vivid imaginations
and whose stories are not reliable, there are others
whom we can believe because we have confidence in
their truthfulness and integrity.*[1]

Latter-day Saints should also be aware that any stories
which have translated beings instructing people to go against
the established doctrines of the Church, or have such translated individuals espousing new doctrines for the Church,
should automatically be dismissed as falsehood; for the Lord
does not operate His kingdom in this manner. Translated
beings only act as "ministering angels" in behalf of the
Lord, to basically bring people to the knowledge of the
truth of the gospel as restored in these latter-days. Any new
doctrine for the Church is always revealed first through the
Lord to His authorized servant upon this earth: the Prophet
and President of The Church of Jesus Christ of Latter-
day Saints.

The author realized that the further away a story becomes from its original source, the greater the chance the
account has of becoming distorted or lacking in specific
details. Therefore, this writer has striven to include only
those accounts that are either first or second generation, or
that seem to be of possible validity and/or historical significance.[2] It is hoped, of course, that those who read these
accounts will seek inspiration for themselves in determining
the truthfulness of the stories contained herein.

An Experience of One of Columbus' Sailors
By E. D. Partridge, of Brigham Young University

Members of The Church of Jesus Christ of Latter-day
Saints are always on the lookout for evidences of the Divine

---

1. *Letter*, dated December 15, 1941 from Joseph Fielding Smith to
Mr. Hector Lee, of the Department of English, University of Utah. A
copy of this letter is in the possession of this author.

2. For further accounts of modern appearances of John the Revelator and/or the Three Nephites, see bibliographical sources listed in the
back of this book under the names of the following authors: Auston
E. Fife, Hector Lee, and William A. Wilson.

origin of the Book of Mormon. This interest led me to mark any passages in Irving's *Life and Voyages of Christopher Columbus*, some of which seem to be worthy of more than a mere passing notice.

Columbus, though steeped in the superstitions of his day, was a very humble man. Often, while sailing abroad, he would spend a whole night in prayer and supplication. He felt that he was doing God's will in making these voyages of discovery; and no doubt, it was this feeling which caused him to say to his officers and men, when implored to return, and even threatened with death, "Sail on—sail on!" Irving says— *(Page 17) "He attributed his early irresistible inclination for the sea, and his passion for geographical studies, to an *impulse from Diety*, preparing him for the high decrees he was *chosen to accomplish.*" And when he came before the king of Spain asking for royal and financial support, "he unfolded his plan with eloquence and zeal; for he felt himself, as he afterwards declared, kindled as with a fire *from on high*, and considered himself the *chosen agent by heaven* to accomplish its grand designs" (page 64). This is very significant when compared with the following: "And I looked and beheld a man among the Gentiles who was separated from the seed of my brethren by the many waters; and I beheld the *Spirit of God* that it *came down and wrought upon the man*, and he went forth upon the many waters, even unto the seed of my brethren who were in the promised land" (I Nephi 13:12).

By far the most interesting paragraph in the whole volume is found beginning on page 329, which I will give.... I have always been deeply interested in the account of the "Three Nephites," and have often wondered if there were not on record somewhere an account of their having been seen by someone outside of the Church. I am almost convinced that Irving had made just such a record....

I will not give the above mentioned paragraph from Irving. It is in the account of Columbus' second voyage of discovery to America. He was cruising along the coast of Cuba, when one day he anchored near a beautiful palm grove:

Here a party was sent on shore for wood and water; and they found two living springs in the midst of the grove. While they were employed in cutting wood and filling their water casks, an archer strayed into the forest with his cross-bow in search of game, but soon returned, flying with great terror, and calling loudly upon his companions for aid. He declared that he had not preceeded far, when he suddenly espied through an opening glade, a man in a long white dress so like a friar of the order of St. Mary of mercy, that at first sight he took him for the chaplain of the admiral. Two others followed in white tunics reaching to their knees, *and the three were of as fair complexions as Europeans.* Behind these appeared many more, to the number of thirty, armed with clubs and lances. They made no signs of hostility, but remained quiet, the man in the long white dress alone advancing to accost him. But he was so alarmed by their number that he had fled instantly to seek the aid of his companions. The latter, however, were so daunted by the reported number of armed natives, that they had not courage to seek them nor await their coming, but hurried with all speed to the ships.

It is stated that Columbus sent two different expeditions in search of the three white men and their followers, but both returned unsuccessful. Irving apologizes for the appearance of this item in his record, and states that, since no tribe of Indians was ever discovered in Cuba who wore clothing, the matter probably arose in either error or falsehood.

No apology is needed, however, by the Latter-day Saints. The account given by the archer portrays conditions just as they would naturally be with the "Three Disciples." They lived among the people when the vision recorded in 1st Nephi was taught. They were, of course, looking forward to its fulfillment. They were to bring souls to Christ till he should come again, and had probably been busy gathering bands of followers all over the country. They, of course, taught their followers to wear clothing and to live as much of the gospel as they could. They naturally would have to arm themselves against their savage neighbors.

Columbus and his sailors were looked upon by the natives as visitors from heaven, and their appearance among them was heralded all over the country. Their movements were watched closely from the shores, since whenever they landed they found themselves not unexpected. It does not take much imagination to see the "disciples" and one of their bands following the movements of the ships from the trees or mountains, awaiting a favorable opportunity to make themselves known. In fact, there is nothing in the report of the archer which is in the least at variance with what might be expected from our knowledge of the Book of Mormon. As I said before, I am almost convinced that this is the record I have been looking for.[1]

The Preparation of a Field
By Lucy Mack Smith

We will now return to Pennsylvania where we left Joseph and Oliver engaged in translating the Record [The *Book of Mormon*, between April-July 1829].

After Samuel left them, they still continued the work as before, until about the time of the proceedings that took place in Lyons, New York. Near this time, as Joseph was translating by means of the Urim and Thummim, he received instead of the words of the Book, a commandment to write a letter to a man by the name of David Whitmer, who lived in Waterloo, requesting him to come immediately with his team, and convey himself and Oliver to his own residence, as an evil-designing people were seeking to take away his (Joseph's) life, in order to prevent the work of God from going forth to the world. The letter was written and delivered, and was shown by Mr. Whitmer to his father, mother, brothers and sisters, and their advice was asked in regard to the best course for him to take in relation to the matter.

---

1. *The Improvement Era, op. cit.*, June 1909, Volume 12, pp. 621-624. *All quotations from Irving in this article are from the works of Washington Irving, *The Life and Voyages of Christopher Columbus* (Peter Fenelon Collier, New York, 1897), Volume 6.

His father reminded him that he had as much wheat
sown upon the ground as he could harrow in two days, at
least; besides this, he had a quantity of plaster of paris to
spread, which must be done immediately, consequently he
could not go, unless he could get a witness from God that it
was absolutely necessary.

This suggestion pleased David, and he asked the Lord
for a testimony concerning his going for Joseph, and was
told by the voice of the Spirit to go as soon as his wheat was
harrowed in. The next morning, David went to the field, and
found that he had two heavy days' work before him. He
then said to himself that, if he should be enabled, by any
means to do this work sooner than the same had ever been
done on the farm before, he would receive it as an evidence,
that it was the will of God, that he should do all in his power
to assist Joseph Smith in the work in which he was engaged.

He then fastened his horses to the harrow, and instead
of dividing the field into what is, by farmers, usually termed
lands, drove around the whole of it, continuing thus till
noon, when, on stopping for dinner, he looked around,
and discovered to his surprise, that he had harrowed in full
half the wheat. After dinner he went on as before, and by
evening he finished the whole two days' work.

His father, on going into the field the same evening,
saw what had been done, and he exclaimed, "There must
be an overruling hand in this, and I think you would better
go down to Pennsylvania as soon as your plaster of paris is
sown."

The next morning, David took a wooden measure under
his arm and went out to sow the plaster, which he had
left, two days previous, in heaps near his sister's house,
but, on coming to the place, he discovered that it was
gone! He then ran to his sister, and inquired of her if she
knew what had become of it. Being surprised she said, "Why
do you ask me? Was it not all sown yesterday?"

"Not to my knowledge," answered David.

"I am astonished at that," replied his sister, "for the
children came to me in the forenoon, and begged of me to

go out and see the men sow plaster in the field, saying, that they never saw anybody sow plaster so fast in their lives. I accordingly went, and *saw three men at work in the field*, as the children said, but supposing that you had hired some help, on account of your hurry, I went immediately into the house, and gave the subject no further attention."

David made considerable inquiry in regard to the matter, both among his relatives and neighbors, but was not able to learn who had done it. However, the family were convinced that there was an exertion of supernatural power connected with this strange occurrence.

David immediately set out for Pennsylvania, and arrived there in two days, without injuring his horses in the least, though the distance was one hundred thirty-five miles. When he arrived, he was under the necessity of introducing himself to Joseph, as this was the first time they had ever met.[1]

A Nephite Visitor
By Mrs. C. E. Edwards

The following circumstance transpired at my home in the Seventeenth Ward, one-half block north of where now stands President Geo. Q. Cannon's house, in April, 1852:

---

1. Lucy Mack Smith, *History of Joseph Smith* (Stevens & Wallis, Inc., Salt Lake City, Utah, 1945; first published in 1853), pp. 147-149. David Whitmer, himself, in a brief statement about the above mentioned event, said to Orson Pratt and Joseph F. Smith 49 years later (in the *Millennial Star*, December 9, 1878, Volume 40, p. 772), that:

> Soon after this, Joseph sent for me to come to Harmony to get him and Oliver and bring them to my father's house. I did not know what to do, so I pressed with my work. I had some 20 acres to plow, so I concluded I would finish plowing and then go. I got up one morning to go to work as usual, and on going to the field, found between five and seven acres of my ground had been plowed during the night. I don't know who did it; but it was done just as I would have done it myself, and the plow was left standing in the furrow.

> Elder Joseph Fielding Smith and others have said on occasions that the men who helped David Whitmer prepare his field were possibly the "Three Nephites." (For example, see footnote number 1 on page 60 within this book.)

I had been to the morning meeting at the Bowery with Sister Dunsdon, she and her little daughter were living with me at this time. My husband was sick at home and in bed. Little Jane, for this was the girl's name, had been left at home to look after my husband's welfare until I should return. As soon as the service was over, I and Sister Dunsdon hastened home. We had scarcely removed our shawls when a knock came at the door. I said, "Come in." The door opened, and to my surprise there stepped in an aged looking gentleman, tall and grave, his hair was as white as wool and combed behind his ears so as to hang down over his shoulders. He wore a felt hat. His pants and coat were dark and considerably worn. His shoes were new, but I noticed that he wore no stockings. His thin features were lit up with a very pleasant smile. When he had entered he said, "Oh, can I have a dinner here today?"

I said, "Yes, indeed! If you can make a dinner of such as I have, you are welcome to it, but I have nothing but bread that I can give you."

I then remembered I had some few onions, and I asked him if he would like some.

He answered, "I would."

I had previously asked him to take a seat. I placed a white cloth on the table, a plate, knife and fork, a glass of water, a plate of bread and a little white dish with four onions. This was the best I could do.

When I had laid the table he turned round to face the table and proceeded to eat. I thought by the way he ate that he must be very hungry.

When he was through he arose from the table, and putting his hand into his pockets said, "What do you charge me for my dinner today?"

I could but smile at the thought of charging for so meager a fare, and said, "Nothing. I am only sorry that I have nothing better to set before you.

With this he said, as he rattled the money in his pocket, "I have plenty of money, and can pay you."

With this he took two or three steps in a measured way towards me, and said, "Well, if you charge me nothing for my dinner, may God bless you, and peace be with you."

There was a power in the voice that I never felt before. I was so overcome by it that my very limbs gave way, and I dropped into my chair. He left, and I told Sister Dunsdon to look after him, to see where he was going. In a minute he disappeared, as though he had left the earth, and not a trace of him could be seen. In those early days there were no houses, not even an outhouse, nor fence of any kind to intercept the eye, and this made us marvel.

I arose myself as soon as my strength returned, but not a thing of him could I see, nor have I seen him since, so far as I know.

But now comes a part of my great surprise, for on turning to clear the table so that we might have a little food ourselves, lo it was all there as I had put it.

This visit of the stranger made a very deep impression on my heart, that has never left me to this day. Some time after this Brothers C. C. Rich and Carrington came to us, as my husband was so very sick. I told them of this visit, and Brother C. C. Rich said, "Sister Edwards, do you know who he was?"

I said, "I do not."

"Well," said Brother Rich, "this was one of the ancient Nephites come to help you in your trouble." Brother Rich knew that I had already seen some trouble.

Afterwards, I met the Prophet Heber C. Kimball and he said the same as Brother Rich had said. Then I enquired no longer in my mind as to who the stranger was. The disguise had been torn away, and my poor heart was made to rejoice exceedingly in that a messenger of God had condescended to grace my humble home with his presence and to bless me there.

All who were here at the time of the famine and are now living remember but too well, how I suffered. I had neighbors all around me who passed three and four weeks without a mouthful of bread. I have administered food to mothers whose babes nursed nothing but blood from their breasts. And to many I gave a little flour and bread, and fed many at my table, yet the Lord in all the famine provided for my family.

I gave in the day of my poverty, of the scanty store I had to the man of God, and it seems that ever after, my meal sack never went empty. The stranger said,

"May God bless you, and peace be with you."[1]

No Footprints
    By Clarissa Young Spencer
    (Daughter of Brigham Young)

During a winter in the early 70's [1870's] my father, President Brigham Young, was planning to take me to Provo to attend Bro. Karl G. Maeser's school. I am not going to tell of the real excitement I got out of the fact I was going on a long trip with Father and the planning by Mother, bless her memory, of my dresses and a coat, etc., to see me through school for the winter. And such pretty dresses they were for those days—a lovely magenta delaine with a broad border braided in black silk braid and a black alpaca dress trimmed with narrow black ribbon velvet. My coat was made of heavy brown woolen material with shoulder cape which was scalloped and bound with brown silk braid with a cap to match of brown velveteen.

We left Salt Lake early one crisp morning, stopping at one of the settlements on the way for lunch. All the people we met seemed happy to have Father stop long enough for lunch and to feed the horses and when we left gave us a great sendoff. That same night we reached Provo where Aunt Eliza gave us a great welcome and a lovely supper, after which we sat in the parlor, talked awhile and relaxed after our day's journey, and then Father and Aunt Eliza called everybody who was in the house to come to the parlor for evening prayers. This was always done. I never left Father's side for a moment (possibly I was a tiny bit home-

---

1. *The Juvenile Instructor, op. cit.,* May 15, 1893, Volume 28, pp. 312-313.

sick for my Mother), until time for bed, then with a good night kiss, I followed Aunt Eliza upstairs. She put me in her bed, after saying my prayers, tucked me in just as Mother always did, and I was too tired to be homesick for long. A feeling of drowsiness soon came over me after sinking down in that lovely feather bed, with the lamp turned low and Aunt Eliza quietly leaving the room. Then oblivion.

Aunt Eliza's home in Provo stood on the northeast corner of one of the main streets. The front of the house faced east. Just opposite, across the street, stood Bishop Smoot's house. Just across the street on the north side stood the tabernacle as it is today. Aunt Eliza's lot was surrounded by a picket fence and a path led from the front door to the main street on the east. On the north side was a porch possibly fifteen feet long in front of the dining room window and door. This room was where we usually sat, as the parlor on the northeast corner of the house was heated and opened only when we had company.

The front hall opened into the dining room and in this hall was the broad staircase which went to the upper floor. This particular winter was very cold with a great deal of snow on the ground. The north door in the dining room we always kept locked and used only the front door on the east. The purpose of this was to get the full benefit of the fire in the stove in the dining room and to keep out as much cold as possible. This is where we studied and practically lived. When I say we I mean Aunt Eliza, Johnnie Walton, a young man from Alpine who worked for his board, and went to Brother Maeser's school, and myself.

This day had been snowing heavily for several hours, but it had cleared up and the sun was shining when I returned from school. I had to break a path from the east gate to the door through six or seven inches of snow. Johnny had remained at school this particular day and consequently not a path had been swept when I returned. It must have been along about four-thirty, for I remember the sun shining through the trees, making the fence, where the snow had piled high, look like it was covered with diamonds.

Aunt Eliza and I were sitting by the fire when a gentle knock came on the north door. We were surprised, as no one ever came to that door. Aunt Eliza motioned me to answer the knock and I got up, feeling perfectly safe as our big watchdog, Rover, lay on the floor beside me. I unlocked the door and opened it and there stood a rather tall man, very pale, wearing a straw hat, blue jacket and spotless blue overalls. "Will you give me something to eat?" he asked. I turned to Aunt Eliza and repeated his question, as he had spoken in a low voice. She invited him to come in and sit down, which he did, placing his hat on the wide window sill. I laid the cloth and we set out a lunch of cold meat, apple sauce, good homemade bread and butter and a pitcher of milk. As the man came to the chair placed for him we went to the other side of the room, Aunt Eliza to her knitting and I to my books. Old Rover raised his head, looked at the stranger peacefully and then dozed off again. This was something unusual for Rover to do for as a rule he was not friendly to strangers.

After awhile the man arose and thanking us in the same subdued voice, picked up his hat and departed, quietly, closing the door behind him. There was something so unusual about the man that I jumped up and ran to the window to have a peek at him. As I passed the table I glanced down and remember distinctly saying breathlessly, "Aunt Eliza, he hasn't eaten anything at all." The food was untouched, aside from a small piece of broken bread. We hurriedly opened the door. The man was nowhere in sight and neither was there a sign of footprints in the newly fallen snow on the porch, on the path leading to the gate or around the house. I ran to the front gate to see if I could see him on the street but he had completely disappeared.

We came back into the house wondering who he was, where he had come from and where he had gone. He was dressed immaculately and his face, with the serene peaceful expression, will remain with me always. Later we made inquiries of our neighbors but none of them had seen or heard of him. Time went on but no explanation developed.

When Father returned, Aunt Eliza related our experience with the stranger and asked, "President Young, what do you think it means?" Father sat for some time twirling his thumbs as was his habit while thinking seriously. I was standing beside him, with his arm around me, waiting anxiously for his reply. As he drew me closer to him, he said very seriously and very quietly, "I believe this house has been visited by one of the Three Nephites." He paused a moment and then said, "We will all kneel and have our evening prayers."

Now just a few more lines to say that I am not trying to convince my readers of the truth of this experience which came to me when I was a child, but had I doubted the correctness of my memory, an incident occurred just a few months ago that has firmly convinced me of the fact that I have neither forgotten nor exaggerated the incident set down in the foregoing statement.

In June of this year, 1930, the telephone operator in the apartment where I live called me to say that there was a gentleman in the lobby to see me. When I went down I immediately recognized, although I had not seen him for fifty years, John Walton, the boy who was living in Aunt Eliza's home the winter the above events took place. We had a very interesting visit talking over old times in Provo and as he was leaving he asked me if I remembered the visit of the strange personage while we were living in Aunt Eliza's home in Provo. When I replied that I remembered it very distinctly he asked me to repeat it to him just as I remembered it and as I have told it here. He told me he had related it to his family many times and it was a great satisfaction to me to know that I had neither added to nor taken away from his recollection of a most interesting occurrence of so many, many years ago.

A picture will always remain in my memory of that peaceful home in Provo: the great big comfortable house, the kindness and thoughtfulness of Aunt Eliza, the unbroken paths of snow surrounding the home on the day of the eventful visit of the stranger and the beautiful influence which I took with me when my dear Father terminated my unusual visit.[1]

An Indian Vision
By G. W. Hill

In a former article I gave an account of my first day's work at baptizing the Indians on Bear River, after they had applied to me so many times to do so. I then promised to give the readers of the Instructor something more on the Indian question, and I shall now tell the reason those Lamanites were impelled to ask for baptism.

Four years ago last summer [1873], some of those Indians were encamped on the south side of Salt Lake, west of Skull Valley, when one day three strange men came into the lodge of the chief, whose name was Ech-up-wy, and after seating themselves commenced talking to him on religious matters. This seemed so strange to him that he turned and scrutinized them closely. *The visitors were evidently Indians, as they had the Indian complexion. One of them was a very large, broad shouldered man, quite good looking; the other two were rather below the medium size.* The large one was spokesman. They told him that the "Mormons' " God was the true God, and that He and the Indians' Father were one; that he must go to the "Mormons," and they would tell him what to do, and that he must do it; that he must be baptized, with all his Indians; that the time was at hand for the Indians to gather, and stop their Indian life, and learn to cultivate the earth and build houses, and live in them. They then said to him "Look!" He turned his head, and, *although he was sitting in his lodge, he saw all this northern country about Bear River and Malad. He saw small farms all over it with grain growing very finely, and small houses dotted here and there all over the land. He saw also that these were Indians' houses, and that there were a great many Indians at work, and apparently feeling first rate.* He noticed also a few white men there showing the Indians how to work, one of whom

---

1. *The Improvement Era, op. cit.,* February 1931, Volume 34, pp. 231-232.

he recognized as myself. What seemed more strange than anything else was that he could see down the canyons on both sides of the mountains, as he might do if he occupied a position in the air above them. After viewing this scene for some time, he turned his eyes in another direction, but not being satisfied he looked around to see more of it, when, to his surprise there was nothing visible before him but the bare side of the lodge. The visitors then told him that when he got his house built and got to living in it, they would come again to see him; they also said something he did not understand, when he turned to ask them an explanation, but, lo! they were gone. His buffalo robes were lying just as they had been, but no visitors were there.

The Indians immediately broke camp and came after me, and wanted me to baptize them, saying that their women and children wanted to be baptized as well as the men, and that it was not good for them to come to Ogden to have the ordinance attended to. They kept importuning for baptism, coming after me as often as once in every week or fortnight until the following spring, when I went and did my first day's work.

Ech-up-wy did not tell me at the first about this vision, nor in fact, any one else; nor could he be made to believe that the place where they are now located was the proper place for them to make farms, although President Young directed that they should locate there, until, when work on the irrigating canal was commenced, he viewed from an eminence the very scene that was shown him in his vision. After that he was satisfied that he was at work in the right place, and told me of his vision, and his reason for demanding baptism.

As to whom the men were who visited Ech-up-wy, the readers can form their own conjecture; but one thing I can say, he has tried as hard to carry out the instructions given him as any man I ever saw. He has now got his house built, as have quite a number of others, and they feel like getting up out of the dirt.[1]

---

1. *The Juvenile Instructor* (An LDS Church magazine), January 1, 1877, Volume 12, p. 11.

Kindness Brings a Restoration in Health
By Mrs. Elzina Robison

It was on a hot summer day in the year 1874, at WaWa Springs in the state of Utah.

The springs being an oasis in the desert, and nothing only sage and bunches of grass and hot sand, it was here in a little lumber shack on their homestead, that Mr. and Mrs. Edwin Squires lived with their three small daughters. They owned horses and cattle and Mr. Squires had two or three men hired to help take care of these animals.

It was on this day in 1874, that they had gone on a roundup, leaving Mrs. Squires and the children alone. They were miles from anyone else and her husband had told her he would be back at a certain time, and to have dinner ready for them. From the house they could see for miles in any direction.

It being about time for them to come back, she went to the spring for water and looked in every direction to see if they were coming, but there was nothing in sight and so she took the water in and set it down and turned around, and there to her amazement was a man standing in the doorway. He asked her if she would kindly give him a bit to eat and although she was frightened she set the table. It was a humble but good meal.

I remember there was cheese, bread, butter, cold milk and an apple pie, and she told him to eat, and that he was welcome. He ate as though he was hungry. While eating he conversed with her and he said: "Sister, you are not well!" And she said: "No, I have had a pain in my shoulder, which has bothered me a great deal." He said: "It is your liver, but you will not be bothered any more with it." Then he got up and started off and thanked her for her kindness and fine meal. He said: "God bless you, Sister, you will never want for anything; you will always be blessed with plenty." He then left. As soon as she thought he had had time to turn the corner of the house, she went out to see in what direction he had gone, but there was no sign of him anywhere. This worried her more than ever. She went back in the house and the conception of Christ, God the Father does not appear. The fertilisation is carried out mysteriously by the Holy Spirit, which intervenes by means of a breath, and takes on the semblance of an angel—or if we look to the iconographical tradition, of a dove. "The achievement of long-distance fertilisation by agency of a messenger, and the choice of an 'airy' way of conception reveal the idea of a tremendous power to which the son is completely subject. The instrument used to translate the fertilisation into action is, however, far from being characteristically virile. Though the dove is obviously a phallic image, it owes its association with love to its gentle and caressing manner of paying court. It must be said, therefore, that this is one of the more effeminate of phallic images! It is thus clear that the power of the Father is only manifested if it is associated with a considerable degree of effeminacy. The same theme is even more evident in the case of the son. He attains grandeur only after having suffered the most profound humiliation, accompanied by a symbolic castration and death. A similar road awaits the followers of Jesus, in the sense that salvation is attained by meekness, humility and submission to the will of the Father."

Exclusion of women from the priesthood is the most obvious aspect of a complex symbolic construction which associates the renunciation of virile powers in the male figure of the priest with the assumption of specifically feminine attributes. Jones notes: "thus obligatory celibacy, the tonsure, and so on, clearly express the deprivation of masculine attributes, and amount to a symbolic self-castration". A specific reference to self-castration can actually be found in the passage from St Matthew (19: 11–12) in which Jesus, talking about the theme of voluntary celibacy, actually says: "Not everyone understands this saying, but only those to whom it has been given. There are eunuchs who have been such since their mothers' breasts, and there are eunuchs who have been made such by other men, but there are also eunuchs who have made themselves such for the sake of the Kingdom of Heaven. Let him who can understand, do so". As we know, there was no lack of cases of all-too-literal interpretation of this passage from the Gospel in the early years of Christianity. The case of Origen is the best-known, but he was certainly not the only one, if we note that the Council of Nicaea concerned itself in 325 with devoting the first of its canons to the subject of self-castration, to exclude from the priesthood those who had had recourse to it in a fit of excessive and misunderstood ascetic zeal. The canon was repeated in various successive Councils, and incorporated into the *Corpus juris canonici*. Self-castration, therefore, was meant to remain purely symbolic, and to be given concrete expression in the ascetic practice of continence, which the Church did not find easy to impose on its clergy. It was only after a good thousand years of permissiveness and tolerance of married priests that the obligation of perpetual continence was definitively imposed by the Second Lateran Council of 1130, as an irrevocable condition of the priesthood. The results were none too satisfactory, for 'right-thinking' people in all times were to protest at the scandal (which lasted about a thousand years and continued until the dawn of our own century) of the obstinate and invincible resistance of a good part of the clergy, in the practice of clerical concubinage.

Literal self-castration—however cruel and barbarous it might appear—at least had the undeniable advantage of resolving a rather difficult and tortuous aspect of asceticism in one neat cut. There can be no doubt whatsoever as to the symbolic significance of continence. A confirmation of Jones' interpretation can in any case be found, clearly stated, in the Jesuit *Dictionnaire de Spiritualité* (II, Paris, 1953, col. 780), which lauds chastity as "the most beautiful of the virtues, because it harmonises in one the most exquisite delicacy which is feminine par excellence, with the energetic mastery of man. To be chaste requires the most uncompromisingly brave efforts by the strongest male forces".

As we can see, we are led inexorably from misogyny to sexophobia; to the rejection of sexuality which is one of the fundamental characteristics of the Christian religion. The rejection of sexuality lays the foundation for an entire hierarchy: the highest crown belongs to virgins who have never practised sex and will never do so—they are the purest and the best. They must act as guides to the others; i.e. the impure who do indulge in sexual practice and thus easily lose the way which leads to the Kingdom of Heaven. In the Christian religion, the rejection of sexuality thus provides its practitioners with a counterbalancing reward—power. On the basis of the distinction between pure and impure, medieval Christianity built the whole model of society which has recently been studied by Georges Duby. The superiority of the clergy, based on their virginity, obviously did not fail to provoke fierce opposition from the powerful laity, and for this very reason they were even less inclined to renounce sexual behaviour. But at the same time it did provide an opening for their womenfolk to seize a small portion of that power which, to their despair, the society of the 'three orders' denied them.

The primacy of continence, and the androgynous compromise which underlies it, was to remain one of the fundamental pillars of christian doctrine in all its forms for many centuries. The Protestant Reformation did not introduce any substantially new element on this point. We can take Luther as typical: the great Rebel of Christendom never at any stage sought to bring the androgynous compromise into his critique of the Catholic tradition. And while he allows the marriage of the clergy, to her surprise the table was just as she had set it, even though she had seen him eat and drink the milk. She then thought how he looked and was dressed so neat; and that his eyes were so bright and just twinkled when he talked; and that he also had a long white beard and his hair was gray.

She was still worrying about what had occurred when her husband and the men came home, and she asked them if they had seen him, but they had not. She told them' the story; and just couldn't get it off her mind. About three months later her mother, Mrs. Abigal Abbott, came to make her a visit and she told her the story. Mrs. Abbott smiled and then said: "Why, Lyda, have you forgot your patriarchal blessing? You were promised that one of the Three Nephites would dine at your table. That's who it was."

Well, she never had any more trouble with her shoulder and lived to a good old age. She always had plenty and her husband died before her; and when she died she left a good start for her children and grandchildren. When she died she was 89 years old.

This story was told to me by my mother, it was about her father's sister, and she heard her tell it; as did Mr. Bowman, who is the father of the family here in our town. He also told the same story.[1]

Indians are Told About the Mormons
By Nephi and S. E. Johnson

The following comes addressed to President Joseph F. Smith:

In the summer of 1876, a personage appeared to the Indians out west of St. George at a place called Duck Creek. *This personage told the Indians that he was one of their forefathers and had many things to tell them, as he had lived*

---

1. Hector Lee, "The Three Nephites: The Substance and Significance of the Legend in Folklore," *Language and Literature* (University of New Mexico, Albuquerque, New Mexico, 1949), Number 2, pp. 17-18. This story was written in 1943 by Mrs. Elzina Robison, Bunkerville, Nevada. Some grammatical errors and usage have been corrected by this author to make the story more easily readable.

Broad and Fifth Streets of Augusta, Georgia. It is locally known as the Pillar of Prophecy.

An interesting story is attached to this old landmark, and it is often recalled from the dusty recesses of memory to impress one with the fundamental truth that God lives and never forgets the utterances of his authorized servants.

The Pillar of Prophecy is a white, concrete shaft, perhaps twelve feet in height. It stands in the center of the sidewalk, the pavement having been laid around it, leaving the Pillar undisturbed. This fact is very significant in that Broad Street is the principal thoroughfare of the city, and space is, therefore, valuable. The significance becomes plain when the story of the Pillar is told.

It is a story that dates back more than thirty years [to about 1890], when Augusta was first catching the glimpse of her present greatness, when she was undergoing the process of transition from a city of the Old South to one of the New. The incident was known then to Augustans, first hand, the old-timers handing it down to their posterity, as a thing worth remembering.

And now for the story. There appeared on the streets of Augusta about thirty years ago a stranger. He was a man of mystery. No one knew whence he came, nor whither he departed. He was a preacher who, like the prophets of old, cried repentance unto the city. *He is described as a man of average height, with hair of pure white and neatly trimmed, stately in appearance, and possessing a voice clear and pleasing, yet incisive, even to the piercing of the human heart.*

This unknown evangelist usually spoke in the Market Place. This was composed of two large sheds, extending about one hundred feet across the street (the street is one hundred and eighty feet from curb to curb), and about two hundred feet long. The sheds were supported by pillars. One shed was known as the "Upper Market," the other the "Lower Market." Here the people of the city gathered each morning to purchase their daily supply of produce from the farmers coming in from the surrounding country.

A remarkable prophecy was made by the Preacher. *He predicted that the "Lower Market" would be destroyed by*

*a storm, but that the southwest corner post would remain
as a testimony to the people that he was a prophet of God,
and that his warning message was true.* He further solemnly
averred that if anyone attempted to move the Pillar that
person would die.

Shortly after the utterance of this strange prophecy, a
devastating electrical storm swept over the city of Augusta,
destroying the "Lower Market" but leaving, as the Prophet
had said, the south-west pillar.

The Piller of Prophecy still stands. No one has ventured
to move it. Neither white nor colored exhibit any willingness
to take the risk. The Pillar also survived the fury of the great
fire of 1916, which practically obliterated the business
district of Augusta. The Pillar escaped unscathed, although
buildings around it are still lying in ruins.

The mysterious Prophet was later entertained at the
home of Mr. and Mrs. Mack Little, of Groveland, Georgia,
which is located about fifteen miles west of Augusta. In con-
versation with Mr. Little, the Prophet reiterated the direful
prediction made on the streets of the city. The Little family
still reside in Richmond County, and vouch for the truth of
the story. They testify that the stranger never divulged his
identity, and that he was never seen again.

Who was this Prophet? Oldtime Augustans believe him
to be John the Baptist, or some other of the Biblical prophets.
But Latter-day Saints are of the belief that the stranger may
have been one of the Three Nephite apostles who were
graciously permitted by the Christ to tarry on the earth until
he should return in glory.

Said the risen Lord to the three apostles, discerning their
desires: "Behold, I know your thoughts, and ye have desired
the thing which John, my beloved, who was with me in my
ministry, before that I was lifted up by the Jews, desired of
me; therefore more blessed are ye, for ye shall never taste of
death, but ye shall live to behold all the doings of the Father,
unto the children of men, even until all things shall be
fulfilled, according to the will of the Father, when I shall
come in my glory, with the powers of heaven; and ye shall
never endure the pains of death; but when I shall come in my

glory, ye shall be changed in the twinkling of an eye from mortality to immortality: and then shall ye be blessed in the kingdom of my Father" (*Book of Mormon*, III Nephi, 28:6-8).

Additional testimony that this prophet may have been one of the Three Nephite apostles was furnished the writer by Patriarch David F. Fawns, of Raymond, Canada. Elder Fawns fulfilled a mission in Georgia, over twenty years ago. On this mission much of his time was spent in Augusta. He testifies that while standing beside the Pillar, *a personage approached and stood before him. Twice this manifestation appeared, and so vividly impressed was he that he can to this day minutely describe the person and his garb. His glorious, radiant countenance* is one that will bless Elder Fawn's memory forever, he declares.

The accompanying cut is an excellent view of the Pillar. The picture was taken in November, 1918, showing the Pillar to be perfectly preserved. It is an object of wonder and curiosity to the people of Augusta in general. To the Latter-day Saints it is especially significant, for it indicates to them that the three ancient American apostles are engaged in ministering among us as the Savior commissioned them to do, centuries ago.[1]

A Wonderful Testimony
By Maud May Babcock

During the summer of 1900, I spent my vacation at Brighton, Silver Lake, Utah. It was the first opportunity I had had to spend any length of time in the mountains and I was so enthusiastic and ambitious that I wanted to climb every peak. Each day I explored some wonderful point around Brighton, on foot and on horseback. Carrie Helen Lamson, a school teacher, some years older than I, was my companion on most of the trips. With each trip we grew more venturesome and went farther from camp.

---

1. *The Improvement Era, op. cit.*, Volume 23, pp. 247-249.

On one ride we explored the canyon beyond Alta, in
Little Cottonwood, and finding ourselves on the pass between
there and American Fork Canyon, we pressed on, hoping to
climb a high peak we could see at the head of the canyon.
Suddenly we realized that the daylight would not permit us
to reach our goal. So we were forced to content ourselves
with climbing the mountain upon which we then were. The
miners called it North Pole Peak. It was much higher than
we thought, and as we gained each height we found yet a
higher point ahead, so that when the top was finally reached,
to our astonishment we were on the very top of the world,
higher than any point around us. Before us was spread the
finest view we had ever seen. Since then I have revisited this
mountain top a number of times and I am always overcome
by the grandeur and extent of the panorama. To the north
and west, over the mountains, lay Salt Lake and Ogden like
toy cities with the Great Salt Lake stretching between like a
great mirror. To the west, between the ridges, was American
Fork Canyon, and Provo Canyon farther south, while behind
to the east was the Provo Valley like a huge checker board.
Near us, nestling in the very tops of the mountain range, we
could count thirteen lakes, while to the east, range upon
range of blue mountains, like great billows of the ocean,
seemed to roll on and on into space. With this view before
us, and with the spirit of adventure within us, I then made a
plan to go further and make a two days' trip over the trail
we had come and on into American Fork Canyon, through
its south fork into Provo Canyon, and to spend a night at
the south fork of the Provo. The second day we could go up
the canyon to Midway and the Hot Pots, and over the mountains back to Brighton.

When we came down North Pole Peak to where we had
been forced to leave our horses, it was near supper time and
we were very hungry. We stopped on the slope at the Albion
Mine, and were more than glad to accept the supper which
the Superintendent of the Mine so kindly offered us when
we passed on our way up the mountain. Being too late for
the regular supper and while the Chinese cook, who took
Miss Lamson for a Salvation Army lassie because of her blue

poke bonnet, prepared the meal, I used an empty nail keg on the dump for a stage and in the twilight, told stories and read Riley to the miners. It was a great enthusiastic audience in that magnificent amphitheatre. The journey back to camp was thrilling, the ride through the pines above Twin Lakes in the moonlight, awesome. A memorable day indeed!

We discussed our plan with those around camp and were told it was feasible. So a week later we started out on horseback. We were directed to take a shorter trail above Dog Lake to Lake Catherine, and to take that divide rather than the longer way over the Alta pass by the Twin Lakes. It is a trail I now know well, but it was new to me then. We reached, as we thought, the trail near a deserted mine dump over Dog Lake about seven o'clock in the morning, but soon could get no farther, nor get back without crossing a crevice filled with shale. I tried to force my horse across, but when the shale began to slide he would not move. Miss Lamson's horse would not make the attempt, and they were farther down the side of the mountain than I was. Seeing that both my horse and I were in danger of sliding down the mountain a thousand or more feet, I dismounted as carefully as I could, in fear for my own life, and that of my horse. I climbed slowly and carefully around the shale bed up to the top of the mountain to look for help, hoping that I might see some stray prospector. But no; although the top was like a lawn sloping in every direction, no one was in sight. Not a living thing to be seen; only the grandeur of the mountains spread before me in the stillness of the early morning. Disappointed, I cautiously climbed over the jagged peak above my horse, and half holding to a small bush with my hands, and half holding by my feet in that sliding shale, I reached down to my horse, almost under me, and touched him with a small willow, trying to coax him across the shale. He would not move. At this crucial moment, fearing the horse would any moment slide down the mountain and I would be dashed to death after him if the shale began to move, I prayed my Heavenly Father for help. As I raised my head a voice above me said, "How did you come here, my daughter?" I jabbered in my relief and excitement, trying to explain our predicament, and before my explanation was finished I was standing on the top, with Miss Lamson and both our horses in a circle facing the stranger. We had no recollection of how we or the horses got there. *The man had a gray Vandyke beard, a cap on his head and was dressed in very new blue overalls.* He was very clean and I was surprised to notice his *white hands as if unused to manual labor.* He addressed me as "My daughter," but although Miss Lamson asked him several questions, he directed his answers always to me instead of to her. I inquired about the road and the way and he said, "Go right on, my daughter, the way you are going, and you will be all right." While talking to him, unconsciously we got on our horses. Before we had gone twenty feet, it came to me I had failed to thank the man who had saved our lives. I turned to atone for my neglect and ingratitude, but although we could see at least a mile in every direction, the stranger had vanished. We seemed to have been in a daze from the wonder and marvel of our experience, which had seemed perfectly natural, when it rushed over me and as inspired, I said, "He was one of the three Nephites."

Miss Lamson was not in the church. She did not even believe in God. In our discussions and arguments and during our readings of Matthew Arnold and Walter Pater, I had explained the Gospel restored, but she could not understand me, nor was she at all interested. She asked me who was a Nephite? And as we rode along that early morning with the spirit of the stranger with us, I explained the Book of Mormon, and told how the Savior, when visiting His people on the American Continent, had granted three Nephite Apostles the blessing bestowed upon John the Beloved, to tarry and preach the Gospel until He should come again. During the next three days, I explained the principles of the Gospel—indeed, we talked of nothing else. As I was talking of the stranger, I suddenly was aware of peculiar hob-nail footprints pointing toward us on the trail. We met the stranger about seven o'clock in the morning, and we followed the footprints always coming to meet us, until we reached the American Fork Canyon, after one o'clock that afternoon. Whenever I thought I could make a short cut, I would be forced to come back to the footprints, for the way would be impassable. When we came down the mountain into the canyon, we met some miners, the first persons we had seen since the stranger left us. They advised us not to go through the South Fork into the North Fork of the Provo, because of deep snow, but to go instead through Deer Creek into Provo Canyon. I should have trusted my stranger, for we found the journey long and tiresome and did not reach camp until after midnight. We lost the footprints when we left American Fork Canyon. I have always believed we would have found the way passable, and that the footprints would have led us over the mountain, and we would have seen the glacier behind Timpanogos, which we had planned to see.

After our night's rest, on very hard beds, we started up the Provo River to the Hot Pots. Because of our clothes (bloomers and trousers were very noticeable on women in those days), we decided to take the north side of the Provo Valley and avoid the towns on the south side. For a mile or so after we came out of the canyon all was well, when suddenly the good road ran out into an irrigation ditch, with large willow trees on either side so dense that we had to lie flat on our horses to avoid the trees, and were forced to drive our horses through the ditch. After going a half a mile or so, my horse suddenly wheeled around, nearly tearing my clothes off by overhanging limbs of the trees. He did the same thing the second time, when Miss Lamson suggested rattlers. Frightened, I got off my horse and peeping around a huge willow trunk, I saw my first rattlesnake, a large one curled up with his head ready to strike. But we decided it would be easier to brave the rattler rather than go back through the awful willows. So gathering up stones, we whipped our horses, throwing stones where the snake was as we passed. We didn't stop to see if they hit. Our horses were so afraid that Miss Lamson's dashed down into the willows, while mine went in the opposite direction up the mountain side into the shale. When the horse began to go up the mountain, sliding with the shale, I slid off his back and I found myself in a hot bed of baby rattlers from six inches to a foot long, hissing and rattling in every direction. I did a

realistic snake dance, rushing over the shale to get away from
the snakes. Finally I went around and met the horse beyond the rattlers and then I discovered my watch and chain
were gone. They were dear to me, being a gift from a friend
who was dead. I had promised not to part with them.

I concluded that when the horse was turning in the
ditch, the willows had torn my jacket open, and broken the
heavy chain, and the watch was back in the ditch near the
big rattler. I must have that watch. I prayed and thereby
gained courage to go back over the shale where the little
rattlers had been, to the tree where we saw the big one. Not
a rattler large or small did I see on my way! The horses had
muddied the ditch so it was impossible to see anything in the
water. I poked about with a stick hoping to catch the chain
and drag it out. After a few terrified minutes in fear of
rattlers, I gave up in despair. Again I prayed and as I opened
my eyes, on a low bush, over which I had been standing
dragging the ditch, was the watch and chain. The watch
cases were open, filled with mud, and the chain was muddy.
With a prayer of gratitude I hurried back to my horse. After
cleaning the mud from the watch, it started to go and kept
as good time as before the accident.

When Miss Lamson and I got through the willows and
shale, we were soon at the Hot Pots Hotel. After a bath in the
pool, in that hot water from the springs, and a fine chicken
and trout dinner, we felt like new beings. I told Miss Lamson
my experience with the watch, and we were both deeply
humbled through our experiences and deep testimony of
the efficacy of prayer. The next day's journey over the
mountains back to Brighton was spent with joy, talking of
the things of the Gospel, and God's wonderful manifestations
to His children in these last days. Our friends welcomed us,
as the whole camp were ready to take up a hunt for us,
fearing we were lost in the mountains.

The spirit, influence and testimony of these three days
in the mountains has remained with me all these years, to
strengthen my faith, the knowledge of God, His works, and
conviction that God answers prayer. Miss Lamson was so
affected by our experience, that there came to her a testi-

mony that we have a Heavenly Father, that He lives and answers individual prayer. She soon after received a testimony of the Gospel and joined the Church.[1]

Missionaries are Protected
By Glen J. Brown

Five years prior to this incident, two "Mormon" elders had been accused of criminally assaulting a young woman on the Island of Vancouver. For some reason they were proved guilty of the charge and sentenced according to the law of the Island. (The Church, as well as the missionaries who were involved, believed that the act was purposely committed by enemies of Mormonism who arranged the evidence in such a way that it was possible to convict the Mormon elders.)

The Church immediately closed the mission and refrained from sending additional elders into that field. Later, when the Church officials believed that the people had partially forgotten the incident, they sent my father and John J. Oldroyd to open the mission [in about 1915]. They found the natives of the Island as hostile toward the Mormons as ever. Everywhere they were looked down upon as potential criminals. People shied away from them.

One evening they decided to hold a street meeting. They knew feeling was running high and that they would probably be molested, but they decided to go ahead regardless. After obtaining a permit from the city officials, who again reminded them of the intolerance of the people, they commenced their meeting. They had little more than started when down the street marched a large group of men and boys carrying several large pots of melted tar and several old feather ticks. The leader walked directly to my father and asked him if he was a Mormon. Much to the satisfaction of the mob, my father answered him in the affirmative.

Some of the members of the mob began to tear open the feather ticks, while others stirred the still warm tar. Just

---

1. *The Juvenile Instructor, op. cit.,* November, 1921, Volume 56, pp. 584-587.

as the mob leader and two or three of the mobsters began to tear the clothes from my father's body, *a white-haired gentleman* (no one saw him arrive at the scene) grasped the leader by the wrists and said in a loud commanding voice, "I have heard these boys preach back in the old country, and they are all right. Now let them alone."

At this the mob leader showed signs of wanting to fight. (The mob leader was a huge, muscular type of man.) Immediately, the newcomer grasped him at the nape of the neck with one hand and by the belt with the other and shook him so soundly, taking him completely off his feet, that when he had finished the mobster could not stand without assistance. Members of his mob picked him up, gathered up their feathers and tar, and departed much faster than they had appeared.

My father and his companion thanked the white-haired man for what he had done and asked him to stay and attend the remainder of the meeting. He accepted their invitation and stood directly in front of them throughout the services. In the meantime, a large crowd had assembled, partly to hear what the elders had to say and partly to get a glimpse of the man who had humbled the mobsters. Eventually the crowd got so large that automobile traffic was completely blocked on the corner where the meeting was being held.

After my father and Mr. Oldroyd had both spoken, and it was time to close the meeting, the white-haired gentleman was still present. All during this time he had stood in identically the same place, scarcely moving. Mr. Oldroyd closed the meeting with prayer, as was the custom, and then looked at the spot where the man had been standing. It was vacant. (This was before anyone in the crowd had moved at all.) No one had seen him go, not even the people who had been standing at his side.

Quite a commotion followed. Members of the crowd were personally questioned as to whether they had seen the man leave or not; no one had even so much as seen him move from the spot.

It seems that someone in the crowd would have seen him leave if he had left in the usual way—by walking.

Remembering that the crowd was large and the people were pushed closely together, also that he had been pointed out and looked at by everyone, it seems strange that no one saw him leave. He would have had to push his way through the crowd in order to depart from the scene, yet he disappeared instantaneously. Many said that they saw him standing in front of the platform during the offering of prayer.

As I understand it, the Nephites are supposed to be able to appear and disappear at will; on this, was based the conclusion that he might have been one of those three.[1]

No Ordinary Stranger
Told by Mr. Niels J. Nielson
to a writer of the FWPA, Utah

In the early evening one day in the autumn of 1928 [in Salt Lake City], an old man came to the corral gate [of Niels J. Nielson] and begged a night's lodging for himself and his team.

"Why yes, sure you can stay here, but we have no hay for the team, but then I think we can get the Bishop to care for them," was the reply of Mr. Niels Joseph Nielson.

After making arrangements with the Bishop, the two men went together into Mr. Nielson's humble home and his wife said, "Niels, you are kind of liberal aren't you, not only letting this man in, but asking the Bishop to feed his team?"

Niels replied, "Now that's all right, mamma."

The stranger seated himself by the fireplace and told them how he had asked at several places for a night's lodging and that in each instance he had been refused. Then he went on to tell what would become of people who were so self-centered that they would not help a man who was in need.

---

1. Auston E. Fife, "The Legend of the Three Nephites Among the Mormons," *Journal of American Folklore* (U.S.A., 1940), Volume 53, pp. 44-46. The author of this story, Glen J. Brown, writes that this was an incident encountered by his father, George E. Brown, and John J. Oldroyd, over twenty-five years ago. The incident occurred on the Island of Vancouver, B.C., Canada.

Moreover, this man made several prophecies which later came true. When this stranger had eaten a supper consisting of bread and milk with the family, the chairs were moved back near the fireplace, and the visitor told of the cities which he had visited all over the world and of the hundreds of miles which he had travelled. As Mrs. Nielson listened to the stories, she thought, "What a blowhard!" Finally she asked, "Have you been in Kansas?" The stranger said that he had, so Mrs. Nielson thought that she would find out how things looked at her old home town. She asked him several specific questions about it and to each the stranger was able to give the correct answer, and able to tell her all that she wanted to know. She was certain that he had really been there.

Having assured herself that this was no ordinary stranger, she started to get up from her chair when she was seized by a severe pain. As she got up and started out of the room the stranger asked her if she was in great pain.

"Yes, I am and have been for quite awhile. They seem to think that I have a cancer."

When he had heard this the stranger addressed her saying, "You will never have pain there any more." Later, when Mrs. Nielson went to the toilet, much to her surprise she passed something which looked like the cancers which are removed by doctors today.

When it came time to go to bed, the twelve-year-old son, who was to sleep at the neighbor's, called his father into another room and said, "Have I got to give up my bed for an old tramp, and maybe he will leave crumbs in it to boot." As the father went back to consult with his wife, he met the stranger who told him to inform his son that he needn't be afraid of crumbs being left in his bed, for, said the stranger, "I am a clean man and I do not want to take his bed."

When everything had been arranged, they settled down and had a good night's rest. An early breakfast was served, but it was noticed that the stranger ate little. When they had finished the meal, Mrs. Nielson asked if he wanted a lunch put up for him and he replied, "That might be all right."

The lunch was soon ready and as he took it, he said, "You will never want for bread." Then he pronounced a blessing on the family and, leading his team, started away down the road.

It was not long before relatives came for a visit, approaching along the same road on which the stranger had departed. Mrs. Nielson asked if they had seen a man leading two horses south on the road they had just come over. They said that they had seen nothing. Then Mrs. Nielson gasped, "For goodness sake! There was no other place for him to go." When the events of the previous evening were enumerated and the whole matter had been discussed, it dawned upon them that this stranger might have been one of the Three Nephites. "How dense of us, we have been kept from seeing. He healed Mother, promised we would never want for bread, said he had travelled a great distance in one day— farther than would be possible for him and his team to go— and made several prophecies, and nothing had impressed us with the fact that he was one of God's travelling messengers." The family affirms that all of the prophecies which he made have come true and that his promise to them has certainly been fulfilled, for since that time they have always had more than they ever did before.[1]

The Lord Aids Israel in Their War of 1948
By Arthur U. Michelson

[Quoted by Elder LeGrand Richards and President Joseph Fielding Smith, as possible evidence of the appearance and intervention of the Three Nephites and John the Revelator on behalf of the Israelis, in their war with the Arabs in 1948.]

---

1. Auston E. Fife, *op. cit.*, pp. 19-21. Fife writes that this story was "retold from a manuscript in the files of the Federal Writers Project, Salt Lake City, Utah, and loaned" to him "through the courtesy of Mr. Charles Madsen. The story was written by an agent of the Federal Writer's Project and verified by Mr. Nielson after writing."

On my recent trip to Palestine I saw with my own eyes how God's prophecy is being fulfilled. In Gen. 17:8, God promised Abraham that he would give this land to him and his seed for an everlasting possession. The Jews waited 2,500 years for the fulfillment of this promise. After World War II, England, which had mandatory power over Palestine, suddenly gave it up and the Jews marched in. This was marvelous, for Palestine was one of the strongest fortresses England had in the Mediterranean Sea. Many contend today that the day of miracles is past, and that God does not intervene any more on behalf of His people, but they have learned through the events in Israel that they were mistaken.

It was marvelous what God did for the Jews, especially in Jerusalem, during the fighting with the Arabs. Though quite a few months had passed since the victory of Israel's army in Israel, they were still talking about what had taken place. Everywhere I went I heard how God had intervened in their behalf, and how He helped them to win the battles. One of the officials told me how much the Jews had to suffer. They had hardly anything with which to resist the heavy attacks of the Arabs, who were well organized and equipped with the latest weapons. Besides, they had neither food nor water because all their supplies were cut off.

The Arabs, who had a great army in strong position, were determined to destroy the Jews, while the Jews were few in number, without any arms and ammunition. The two or three guns they possessed had to be rushed from one point to another, to give the Arabs the impression that they had many of them. The Jews had quite a few tin cans which they beat as they shot the guns, giving the impression of many shots. But as the pressure was too great, they were unable to hold the lines any longer and finally decided to give up the city. At this critical moment God showed them that He was on their side, for He performed one of the greatest miracles that ever happened. The Arabs suddenly threw down their arms and surrendered. When their delegation appeared with the white flag, they asked, *"Where are the three men that led you, and where are all the troops we saw?"* The Jews told them that they did not know anything of the three men, for this group was their entire force. *The Arabs said that they saw three persons with long beards and flowing white robes, who warned them not to fight any longer, otherwise they would all be killed.* They became so frightened that they decided to give up. What an encouragement this was for the Jews, who realized that God was fighting for them.

God performed the same miracles on other fighting fronts, for He wanted to show the nations that He had turned to the Jews again, and like in the olden days, would help them to conquer the land. The Arabs were especially strong in the Negev District, not far from Beersheba, for they were backed by a large Egyptian army. The Jews were encircled by the Egyptians, and humanly speaking, had absolutely no chance to escape. One morning, to the amazement of the Jews, the Arabs and the Egyptians suddenly gave up the fighting and surrendered. The Jews were at first very skeptical, because they couldn't believe that the Arabs and Egyptians would give up their strong position and surrender. But when they saw how the Arabs threw down their arms, they learned that God had intervened for them. When they asked the Arabs and Egyptians for the cause of their surrender, they told them that *they saw an old man with a long beard who was dressed in a white robe,* and who warned them not to fight any longer, otherwise they would all perish. This man was seen and heard by almost all the enemy troops. A great fear came over them and they decided to give up the fight. These and other stories I heard from various Jews who fought on the battle fronts. They said to me, "If God had not intervened, we would all have been killed. We could never have conquered Palestine because we were so few and without arms and ammunition.[1]

---

1. Arthur U. Michelson, *The Jewish Hope* (a periodical, Los Angeles, California, 1950), Issue Number 9, Volume 22, September, 1950.

LeGrand Richards, *Israel, Do You Know* Deseret Book Company, Salt Lake City, Utah, 1954), pp. 229-233.

Joseph Fielding Smith, *The Signs of the Times* (Deseret News Press, Salt Lake City, Utah, 1952), pp. 227-229.

SELECTED BIBLIOGRAPHY

Andrus, Hyrum L., *Doctrines of the Kingdom* (Bookcraft, Inc., Salt Lake City, Utah, 1973), 576 pp.

Book of Mormon, The (The Church of Jesus Christ of Latter-day Saints, 1968 ed.), 568 pp.

Brigham Young University Speeches of the Year; Provo, Utah. An annual publication.

Brigham Young University Extension (Service) Publication; Provo, Utah, January 5, 1965.

Burton, Alma P., *Doctrines From the Prophets* (Bookcraft, Inc., Salt Lake City, Utah, 1970), 476 pp.

Church News (of The Church of Jesus Christ of Latter-day Saints), section of the Deseret News: a daily newspaper (Salt Lake City, Utah, 1943-1975).

Clark, James R., *Messages of the First Presidency* (Bookcraft, Inc., Salt Lake City, Utah, 1965), Volumes 1-5.

Conference Reports (Annual and Semi-annual of The Church of Jesus Christ of Latter-day Saints, 1897-1975).

Crowther, Duane S., *Life Everlasting* (Bookcraft, Inc., Salt Lake City, Utah, 1967), 399 pp.

Doctrine and Covenants, The (The Church of Jesus Christ of Latter-day Saints, 1968 ed.), 312 pp.

Ensign, The (Monthly magazine of The Church of Jesus Christ of Latter-day Saints, 1970-1975).

Fife, Auston E., "The Legend of the Three Nephites Among the Mormons," *Journal of American Folklore* (U.S.A., 1940), Volume 53, pp. 1-49.

First Presidency of The Church of Jesus Christ of Latter-day Saints, The, *Gospel Doctrine: Selections from the Sermons and Writings of Joseph F. Smith* (Deseret News Press, Salt Lake City, Utah, 1971), Volumes 1-2.

First Presidency of The Church of Jesus Christ of Latter-day Saints, The, *Immortality and Eternal Life: Selections from the Writing and Messages of President J. Reuben Clark, Jr.* (Deseret News Press, Salt Lake City, Utah, 1969), 338 pp.

Friend, The (Monthly magazine of The Church of Jesus Christ of Latter-day Saints, 1970-1975).

Gospel in Principle and Practice, The (Brigham Young University Press, Provo, Utah, 1966), Volumes 1-2.

Holy Bible, The (Old and New Testaments—King James Edition, Missionary copy bound for The Church of Jesus Christ of Latter-day Saints, 1969 ed.).

Improvement Era, The (Monthly magazine of The Church of Jesus Christ of Latter-day Saints, 1897-1970).

Inspired Version of the Bible (Reorganized Church of Jesus Christ of Latter-day Saints, Herald Publishing House, Independence, Missouri, 1944), 1,576 pp.

Instructor, The (Monthly magazine of The Church of Jesus Christ of Latter-day Saints, 1930-1970).

Journal History of the Church (Items about The Church of Jesus Christ of Latter-day Saints; a historical collection since the mid-1800's: available at the Church Historian's Office, Salt Lake City, Utah).

Journal of Discourses (Contains talks given by General Authorities and other Church leaders of the LDS Church between the years 1851-1886).

Juvenile Instructor (Monthly magazine of The Church of Jesus Christ of Latter-day Saints, 1866-1929).

Kimball, Spencer W., *Faith Precedes the Miracle* (Deseret Book Company, Salt Lake City, Utah, 1972), 364 pp.

Kimball, Spencer W., *The Miracle of Forgiveness* (Bookcraft, Inc., Salt Lake City, Utah, 1969), 376 pp.

Lee, Harold B., *Stand Ye In Holy Places* (Deseret Book Company, Salt Lake City, Utah, 1974), 398 pp.

Lee, Hector, "The Three Nephites: A Disappearing Legend," *American Notes and Queries* (June, 1942), Volume 2, Number 3, pp. 35-38.

Lee, Hector, "The Three Nephites: The Substance and Significance of the Legend in Folklore," *Language and Literature* (University of New Mexico, Albuquerque, New Mexico, 1949), Number 2.

McAllister, Dale A., "An Analysis of Old Testament Chronology in the Light of Modern Scripture and Scientific Research" (*Thesis*, Brigham Young University, Provo, Utah, 1963), 193 pp.

McConkie, Bruce R., *Doctrines of Salvation: Sermons and Writings of Joseph Fielding Smith* (Bookcraft, Inc., Salt Lake City, Utah, 1954), Volumes 1-3.

McConkie, Bruce R., *Mormon Doctrine* (Bookcraft, Inc., Salt Lake City, Utah, 1966), 856 pp.

Michelson, Arthur U., *The Jewish Hope* (a periodical, Los Angeles, California, September, 1950), Issue Number 9, Volume 22.

Millennial Star, The (Monthly magazine of The Church of Jesus Christ of Latter-day Saints, Great Britain, 1840-1970).

New Era, The (Monthly magazine of The Church of Jesus Christ of Latter-day Saints, 1970-1975).

Newquist, Jerreld L., *Gospel Truth: Discourses and Writings of President George Q. Cannon* (Deseret Book Company, Salt Lake City, Utah, 1957), Volumes 1-2.

Pearl of Great Price, The (The Church of Jesus Christ of Latter-day Saints, 1968 ed.), 65 pp.

Pratt, Orson, edited by, *The Seer* (Liverpool, England, 1853-1854), Volumes 1-2, 320 pp.

Relief Society Magazine, The (Monthly magazine of The Relief Society of The Church of Jesus Christ of Latter-day Saints, particularly 1914-1964).

Richards, Franklin D., and Little, James A., *A Compendium of the Doctrines of the Gospel* (1898 edition).

Richards, LeGrand, *A Marvelous Work and a Wonder* (Deseret Book Company, Salt Lake City, Utah, 1969 ed.), 452 pp.

Richards, LeGrand, *Israel, Do You Know* (Deseret Book Company, Salt Lake City, Utah, 1954), 252 pp.

Roberts, Brigham H., *A Comprehensive History of the Church* (Brigham Young University Press, Provo, Utah, 1956), Volumes 1-6.

Smith, Joseph *(The Documentary) History of the Church* (Deseret Book Company, Salt Lake City, Utah, 1946-1951), Volumes 1-7.

Smith, Joseph F., *Gospel Doctrine* (Deseret Book Company, Salt Lake City, Utah, 1919), 553 pp.

Smith, Joseph Fielding, *Answers to Gospel Questions* (Deseret Book Company, Salt Lake City, Utah, 1957), Volumes 1-6.

Smith, Joseph Fielding, *Teachings of the Prophet Joseph Smith* (Deseret News Press, Salt Lake City, Utah, 1938), 408 pp.

Smith, Joseph Fielding, *The Signs of the Times* (Deseret News Press, Salt Lake City, Utah, 1952), 240 pp.

Smith, Lucy Mack, *History of Joseph Smith* (Stevens & Wallis, Inc., Salt Lake City, Utah, 1945; first published in 1853), 355 pp.

Talmage, James E., *Jesus The Christ* (Deseret Book Company, Salt Lake City, Utah, 1961 ed.), 804 pp.

Talmage, James E., *The Articles of Faith* (Deseret Book Company, Salt Lake City, Utah, 1961 ed.), 536 pp.

Teachings of the Living Prophets (Brigham Young University Press, Provo, Utah, 1970), 323 pp.

Widtsoe, John A., *Discourses of Brigham Young* (Deseret Book Company, Salt Lake City, Utah, 1954), 497 pp.

Widtsoe, John A., *Priesthood and Church Government* (Deseret Book Company, Salt Lake City, Utah, 1967 ed.), 397 pp.

Wilson, William A., "Mormon Legends of the Three Nephites Collected at Indiana University" (Brigham Young University Special Collections, Brigham Young University, Provo, Utah). See also the "Folklore Collections" of the English Department at Brigham Young University.

INDEX

W